The Impact of Inflation on
Financial Activity in Business

THE IMPACT OF INFLATION ON FINANCIAL ACTIVITY IN BUSINESS
with Applications to the U.S. Farming Sector

Yaaqov Goldschmidt, Tel Aviv University
Leon Shashua, Agricultural Bank of Israel
Jimmye S. Hillman, University of Arizona

Rowman & Littlefield
PUBLISHERS

ROWMAN & LITTLEFIELD

Published in the United States of America in 1986
by Rowman & Littlefield, Publishers
(a division of Littlefield, Adams & Company)
81 Adams Drive, Totowa, New Jersey 07512

Library of Congress Cataloging in Publication Data

Goldschmidt, Yaaqov.
  The impact of inflation on financial activity in
business, with applications to the U.S. farming sector.

  Bibliography: p. 175
  Includes index.
  1. Agriculture—Economic aspects—United States.
2. Inflation (Finance)—United States. I. Shashua,
Leon. II. Hillman, Jimmye S., 1923–   . III. Title.
HD1761.G645 1986   338.1′3′0973   85-14196
ISBN 0-8476-7427-4

86 87 88 / 10 9 8 7 6 5 4 3 2 1
Printed in the United States of America

CONTENTS

of Interest in Measuring Operating Income, *117;*
9.4 Determining Operating Income, *120;*   9.5 Capital Gains
and Holding Gains, *123;*   Notes, *124;*   Appendix: Treatment
of Equity Additions and Income Withdrawals, *125*

TABLES AND FIGURES

FOREWORD

The decade 1975–85 was an era fraught with dynamic change in respect to the monetary parameters that characterize an industrial economy. Changes in interest rates, asset composition, pricing policies, financial liquidity and taxation, capital formation, and inflation, along with other phenomena, compose a set of factors which introduced a "new situation" in the economies of the United States and other developed countries. This anomalous set of circumstances also resulted in many uncertainties which affect economic growth, employment, and decision-making by managers at the level of the industrial firm.

In no other sector has this new situation affected outcome more than in agriculture. As one who was intimately involved with management and decision-making in an agribusiness firm during the 1970s, I can attest to the overriding importance of the macroeconomic factors which impinged on my daily decisions. Both as manager and as part owner, I encountered incidents during this period which had never before arisen with respect to their nature and level of intensity. For example, it was the inflation of the late 1970s and 1980–81 which distorted asset values in agriculture and which, along with other factors, resulted in the crisis—the disaster—witnessed at the farm level in the mid-1980s. Agribusinesses, banks, and all of agriculture suffered.

Could anything have been done by farmers and others associated with the agricultural sector to have avoided this disaster? Can anything be done to assuage its impact should it reoccur? While these questions cannot be answered with complete and positive assurance, research evidence now available provides us with tools that will make the answers easier to obtain. In their book, Professors Goldschmidt, Shashua, and Hillman address the evidence and provide analyses which portend a brighter aftermath should such economic "storms" again arise.

In my opinion, this book will be of particular assistance to those farmers and other businessmen who have in the past incorrectly treated interest expense in conducting their financial analyses under conditions of persistent inflation. Other observations could be made. For example, to eliminate or avoid equity erosion and financial stress during inflation, a businessman must reconstruct his loans. The authors recommend that short-term loans that finance fixed assets be converted to long-term indexed loans. Many other implications for policy are outlined in this excellent text.

The ultimate accolade for an administrator is to be asked to read research results which are applicable to both theoretical and applied problems. This book, a product of a United States-Israel Binational Agricultural Research and Development Fund (BARD) grant, proves once again that well-thought-out projects warrant funding because of their high payoff. I am most happy to encourage the application of the principles outlined by the authors herein.

Bartley P. Cardon
Dean, College of Agriculture
University of Arizona, Tucson

PREFACE AND ACKNOWLEDGMENTS

This book represents the final exposition of a two year research project directed toward analyzing the impact of inflation on financial aspects of business activities, at both the firm and industry levels. The publication is thus intended to serve a wide audience of firms, professionals, and policymakers, especially in the field of agriculture.

Studies of financial analysis under inflation are not new, and much has been published on the subject. Yet, many conclusions arrived at by using the existing analytic procedures at the level of the individual· firm are inconsistent with reality at the level of the entire industry, or of particular sectors. An example is the case of business taxation and earnings: Business income is taxed on a nominal basis; thus inflation is expected to lead to overtaxation of business firms, to an erosion in equity, and to a decline in real earnings. In reality, however, in many countries which suffer from persistent inflation, the tax share taken from business declines considerably, while capital gains and equity show a real increase—thus inflation tends to accelerate. Another notable example is the negligible importance given thus far by many analyses to financial liquidity and to its effect on the activities of business firms during inflation.

The failure to draw correct conclusions at the level of the business firm which are consistent with the sector's reality, as well as the lack of consistent results between ex-post and ex-ante activities, lie mainly in the fact that the role of the interest rate, in particular, and the liability side of the balance sheet, in general, have been treated at variance with the costs and the assets side of the balance sheet. This subject is the theme of our current volume.

The first chapter, which is devoted to the specific role that interest plays in the financial activities of business during inflation, explains the theoretical background needed to develop and fully understand the procedures delineated in subsequent chapters. A detailed application to the United States farm sector for the period 1950–1982 follows each part. The final chapter is devoted to policy implications.

The first part of the book is devoted to determining the interest charges on working capital—a subject that plays a key role in financial analysis under inflation and which has been, until now, neglected in the literature. The effect of debt finance on the future liquidity position of the firm is analyzed in the second part, which is, in turn, followed by an analysis of the impact of inflation on tax liability that results from interest on loans. The third part of the book is a thorough treatment of income measurement, emphasizing the correct procedure for estimating operating income for performance evaluation.

This research was supported by a grant from the United States-Israel Binational Agricultural Research & Development Fund (BARD); it was carried out at the Center for Agricultural Research, Rehovot, Israel, and at the Department of Agricultural Economics, University of Arizona, Tucson.

Thanks are due to Barbara Beard for efficient typing, to Genevieve Gray for editing the manuscript, and to Asaf Goldschmidt for help with computer data processing.

The Impact of Inflation on
Financial Activity in Business

ONE

INTRODUCTION:
THE SPECIFIC ROLE OF INTEREST EXPENSE IN FINANCIAL ANALYSIS UNDER INFLATION

Applying conventional tools of financial analysis to firms' activities under conditions of inflation using deflated data usually leads to incorrect conclusions because tax rules and financing practices are not fully adapted to inflation. Adjusted procedures for inflation accounting, costing, and pricing contain many pitfalls resulting particularly from the incorrect treatment of the interest expense.

In the present chapter,[1] the theoretical models on which this book is based are developed. The models emphasize the specific role that interest plays in financial and economic analysis under inflation. The main impacts of inflation on financial activities of business are also briefly described.

1.1 PROBLEMS FOSTERED BY INCORRECT SPECIFICATION OF THE ROLE OF INTEREST

In times of stable prices, the timeliness of cash flow is handled by the present value technique, using the after-tax cost of capital. During inflation, on the other hand, the relevant discounting rate depends on the pattern of cash flow associated with the type of asset that generates it. The relevant discounting rate will be shown to be, in cases of fixed assets, the pre-inflation rate, and in other cases, the nominal inflation-compensated rate.[2]

During a period of inflation, there are at least two kinds of cash flow. The first, which is typical of monetary assets, is fully inflation-compensated. In this case, cash flow incorporates the inflation of both principal and interest. The second kind, which is typical of fixed assets, consists of returns growing with inflation—as contrasted with inflation on the principal, which is not realized until the asset is sold. Applying the present value technique for discounting the cash flow over the whole lifespan of the asset, using the inflation-compensated rate h, will yield the correct value for both cash flows. This procedure has already been well established. A problem arises, however, when the annual income is estimated.

For discounting the first kind of cash flow, which is generated by monetary assets, the nominal rate should be applied to the nominal cash flow. For discounting the second kind of cash flow, which is generated by fixed assets, there are two possibilities: (1) applying the pre-inflation rate to the cash flow, or (2) adding the inflation-appreciation of the asset to the cash flow and then applying the nominal rate. The above simple rule is often misused by business firms and nearly always by the income tax authorities, as will be illustrated below.

Firms misuse the above rule by applying the nominal rate to cash flows of fixed assets, disregarding the inflation-appreciation of the assets. This disregard is based on the ground that nonrealizable items should not be considered as income by a going concern. This practice yields understated income in a period of inflation. The consequence is that the firm concludes and convinces itself and others, including the government, that it should raise the price of its commodities beyond the inflation factor, leading to double counting of the inflation factor in costing and pricing of asset services and consequently intensifying the overall inflationary process.

Tax authorities, reasoning in a similar way, tax income on the same magic principle of the going concern. The tax distortion resulting from this procedure reflects the particular combination and types of assets and finance (equity or loans) involved. The tax situations discussed in this work are:

	Equity	Debt
Monetary assets	Overtaxation	Neutral
Fixed assets, depreciable	Overtaxation	Undertaxation
Fixed assets, non-depreciable	Neutral	Undertaxation

Prevailing financing and tax procedures tend, by implication, to encourage the following results: (1) deterioration of the firms' financial liquidity resulting from the use of debt in financing investments; (2) double counting the inflation factor in pricing as a result of negative cash flows in new investments; (3) undertaxation of income from fixed assets creating a haven for tax sheltering, which occurs when such assets are financed by loans; and (4) a rise in interest rates required by lenders to overcome taxation as implied by the Darby effect (1975) or due to the effects of government borrowing to balance budget deficits resulting from undertaxation.

The firms' operations are based on several types of assets financed by both equity and loans, and a correct allocation of income and costs associated with these assets is seldom straightforward or clearcut. What is needed are analytic procedures that correctly incorporate the role of interest in income measurement, costing, and pricing, and in investment evaluation concerning the effect of debt financing on the financial position.

1.2 THE ROLE OF INTEREST IN ASSET CLASSIFICATION

During a period of inflation the pattern of cash flow depends on the type of asset generating the returns, as mentioned in section 1.1. The cash flow either includes full inflation-compensation on the principal or it includes only that part of the principal consumed in the analyzed period. Consequently, during inflation there is a question regarding the proper rate to be used for discounting—the pre-inflation real rate or the inflation-compensated rate. In other words, the proper discounting rate should correspond to the type of asset which generates the cash flow. For this purpose, the assets are here classified according to three types, monetary, revolving, and appreciable—corresponding to two types of discounting rates, nominal and real.

Monetary Assets

As the name implies, monetary assets are money items such as cash, receivables, bank deposits, and payables, usually listed in the balance sheet as current assets and liabilities. The cash flow generated by these assets includes partial or full inflation-compensation on the outstanding principal. In this analysis, we assume that the cash flow is fully inflation-compensated according to Fisher; relaxing this assumption will not change the conclusions regarding the proper discounting rate.

Let the firm's required discounting rate (that is, the internal rate of return) be r. Then, for an initial perpetuity investment of one dollar, the present value of returns should equal the initial cost of the investment. In other words, the present value of the perpetual cash flow yielding i per period, under inflation at rate p, is

$$\int_0^\infty \frac{(i + p)}{e^{rt}} \; dt = 1 \tag{1.1}$$

This integral yields $\dfrac{i + p}{r} = 1$

that is, $r = i + p$.

The required discounting rate r is equal to the inflation-compensated discounting rate. In other words, monetary income should be evaluated using nominal discounting rates. The preceding relation offers a formal proof for an obvious fact. It is given here to relate and compare it to the other two types of assets.

Revolving Assets

A revolving asset is one which is continuously consumed and converted into goods. A typical example is working capital needed for operations such as inventory of raw materials, goods in process, and finished goods. The return of such assets in a period of inflation is inflation-compensated and, in principle, the appreciation of the principal is realized during the analyzed period. During inflation, the periodic return grows by the inflation factor.

Specifically, the present value of the perpetual cash flow of a revolving asset in a going concern is

$$\int_0^\infty \frac{(i + p)}{e^{rt}} \; dt = 1 \tag{1.2}$$

where i = the pre-inflation return (not including any asset appreciation).

This integral yields $\dfrac{i}{r - p} = 1$

that is, $r = i + p$.

Table 1.1   Income Statement for a Revolving Asset

A. Relevant data		
Opening inventory, 100 units, worth		$ 100
Purchases during the year		1,000
Sales during the year		1,000
Closing inventory, 100 units, worth		120
Interest expense		20
Loan balance, end of year		120
B. Income statement		
Sales		$1,000
Costs:		
Opening inventory	$ 100	
Purchases	1,000	
Less: closing inventory	(120)	
Interest expense	20	
Total cost		1,000
Net income		–

In other words, the revolving assets behave, for analysis purposes, the same way as monetary assets. The income from revolving assets, as in the case of monetary assets, should be considered as real income and taxed accordingly. All the interest expense actually paid and/or imputed on equity, using an inflation-compensated cost of capital, should be considered as a real cost of production.

Consider the following simple situation, where the rate of interest is 20 percent and is equal to the inflation rate. The opening inventory is 100 units, worth $100, financed by a loan. Additional data and the income statement are presented in table 1.1.

The example illustrates the fact that the $100 capital invested in inventory should be charged the 20 percent nominal rate of interest and not the real rate, which in this case is zero.

Charging real interest on assets used for working capital is a common error incorporated in many analyses. Alternatively, the rate of return on the market value of the revolving assets is not in real terms but rather in nominal terms. To calculate the real rate, the inflation rate should be deducted from this nominal rate of return.

Appreciable Assets

As the name implies, appreciable assets are assets whose values change in accordance with the changes in the price level. These assets are usually recorded in the balance sheets as fixed assets, such as property, buildings, equipment, and stocks in subsidiary companies. The return on these assets is inflation-compensated, and the value of the asset is appreciated in accordance with some specific price level.

In the general case, let the depreciation rate be of the exponential type at the rate of b, and the gross return be $(i + b)$. The gross return under inflation is assumed to grow periodically by the factor e^{pt} where p is the relevant price level change. The present value of the cash flow over the lifespan of the asset, assuming that the returns are reinvested in the same type of asset, is

$$\int_0^\infty \frac{(i + b)e^{pt} \cdot e^{-bt}}{e^{rt}} \, dt = 1 + \int_0^\infty \frac{pe^{pt} \quad e^{-bt}}{e^{rt}} \, dt \tag{1.3}$$

The term on the right is the appreciation value of the asset due to inflation in year t.

This integral yields $\dfrac{i + b}{r - p + b} = 1 + \dfrac{p}{r - p + b}$

Solving for r, we receive the condition $r = i$.

The proper discounting rate is the pre-inflation rate. To put it differently, the asset should be charged the real interest rate or the real cost of capital. The above result holds for any other depreciation scheme and lifespan because the depreciation can be considered as withdrawal of capital and because of the assumption that returns are reinvested in the same type of asset.

Consider a $100 investment in a two-year depreciable asset with zero salvage value and straight-line depreciation. The pre-inflation interest rate is 5 percent and is equal to the firm's discounting rate. The inflation rate is 20 percent and the inflation-compensated interest rate is 26 percent. It is assumed that profits above the imputed earnings (real return of 5 percent and current cost depreciation) are not retained in the firm and are distributed as dividends. The relevant calculations, under both stable prices and inflationary conditions, are presented in table 1.2.

The example illustrates the fact that the $100 capital invested in fixed assets should be charged the 5 percent real interest rate in conjunction with real depreciation charges. Alternatively, the 26 percent nominal interest rate can be charged in conjunction with historical depreciation.

It should be emphasized that the treatment of the appreciable assets is diametrically different from that of the revolving assets. The

Table 1.2   Evaluation of Investment in Appreciable Assets

Year (end)	0	1	2
A. Stable price conditions			
Interest, 5%		$ 5.00	$ 2.50
Depreciation		50.00	50.00
Total charges		55.00	52.50
Present value, 5%	$100.00		
B. Inflationary conditions			
Price index	100	120	144
Case 1:			
Interest, 5%		6.00	3.00
Depreciation, revalued		60.00	72.00
Total		66.00	75.00
Present value, 26%	$100.00		
Case 2:			
Interest, 26%		$26.00	$13.00
Depreciation, revalued		60.00	72.00
Total		86.00	85.00
Present value, 26%	$121.79		
Case 3:			
Interest, 26%		$26.00	$13.00
Depreciation, historical		50.00	50.00
Total		76.00	63.00
Present value, 26%	$100.00		

former should be charged real interest, whereas the latter should be charged nominal interest. The immediate result of this finding is that these two types of assets should not be aggregated into one item in financial analyses such as costing, estimating production functions, and in deflating time series.[3]

1.3 THE ROLE OF INTEREST IN INCOME MEASUREMENT AND PRICING

Recognizing the proposed asset classifications with their respective discounting rates dictates the correct procedures for income measurement. Furthermore, common errors in analyses and practices used under inflation can be pinpointed and corrected. In the following section we will delineate the required procedure for periodic income measurement for an individual investment and for a firm and point out some common pitfalls encountered by businessmen and professionals.

The Case of Individual Investment

Under the assumption of neutral inflation on prices, and ignoring the tax effect (see next section), the economic evaluation of an investment leads to the same conclusion whether the prices are stable or changing. However, net cash flow is greatly affected by the process of inflation. The reason for this is that the periodic earning of the investment grows by the inflation factor—that is, $E_t = E_o (1+p)^t$. Interest on the loans, on the other hand, is supposed to carry inflation-compensation on the principal as well as on interest and is constant over the term of the loan, assuming constant uniform inflation.

For an investment fully financed by a loan, when both have a lifespan of n, the cash inflow and the loan's service is demonstrated by figure 1.1, which shows a negative net cash inflow from the investment in early periods of its lifespan (see chapter 5).[4] Although the investment is balanced over its lifespan, negative cash flow will lead price setting firms to increase prices of their commodities beyond the inflation rate in order to reduce negative cash flow; this pricing process necessarily leads to double counting of the inflation factor. A formal proof is provided below for a revolving asset.[5]

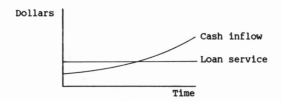

Fig. 1.1 Cash flows of an investment

The return from a one-dollar investment in a revolving asset should be i per period, indexed. Instead, the firm charges i + p in the first year, and raises it by the factor 1 + p in subsequent periods. The present value of the perpetual cash flow stream is

$$\int_0^\infty \frac{(i + p)}{e^{rt}} \, dt = 1 \tag{1.4}$$

where r = discounting rate under zero profit (internal rate of return),
i = pre-inflation rate of return.

$$\frac{i + p}{r - p} = 1$$

that is, $r = i + 2p$.

In practice, only a portion of a firm's investments are ever financed by loans, and only part of the lifespan produces a negative cash flow. Thus double counting could only occur in an extreme case. Although figure 1.1 illustrates an extreme case of 100 percent leverage, it nevertheless indicates conditions at the margin. It is expected, therefore, that the final price will tend more toward the double-counting case than otherwise, especially in a growing firm.

Let us mention that the phenomenon of double counting the inflation rate has been noted by Modigliani and Cohn (1979) in explaining the behavior of investors in setting prices in the stock market during inflation. Moreover, in time of inflation, costing and pricing practices which lead to double counting inflation is a common phenomenon in real life and not a theoretical one.[6]

The Case of a Firm

In measuring the operating income of a firm during inflation, the profit is usually determined after adjusting the depreciation and after charging all the interest expenses actually incurred (for example, U.S. Department of Agriculture, 1983). In section 1.2, it has been shown that loans financing fixed assets should be charged the real interest rate. Thus, the existing income measurement procedures provide underestimated income from operations and overestimated income from capital gains.[7] The correct procedure implied by the asset classification (section 1.2) is to charge nominal interest on working capital (actually paid or imputed on equity) and real interest on loans financing appreciable assets (mostly fixed assets). Formally, the income relation for operating income OI (see chapter 9), should be

$$OI = S - C - I_C - I_F + \Delta\ INV \qquad (1.5)$$

where S = sales
      C = cost as conventionally recorded but including depreciation on current value of assets,
      I_C = imputed interest on working capital, using the nominal market interest rate,
      I_F = imputed interest on loans financing fixed assets, using inflation-free interest rate,

Δ INV = change in current values of inventories less change in historical values of inventories.

The purpose of isolating the operating income from total income (operating income plus capital gains) is to provide an objective criterion for performance evaluation, regarding the variables under the control of the firm. For this reason, we suggest including imputed interest on equity used to finance working capital, in order to facilitate comparisons among firms and over periods of time.

1.4 THE ROLE OF INTEREST IN FINANCIAL LIQUIDITY AND TAXATION

It is a known fact that during inflation, the prevailing income tax rules cause equity erosion. Only scant attention has been given in the literature to the effect of debt (interest expenses) on taxation during inflation.[8] The analysis in chapter 7 indicates that leveraged firms not only can eliminate the erosion of equity but may have a net inflation tax benefit. This phenomenon provides an incentive to increase financial leverage, thereby worsening the firm's financial position. The analysis in chapters 5 and 6 shows that even when financial leverage is kept constant, the effect of inflation on interest expense causes deterioration in the firm's financial liquidity.

The interest rate under conditions of inflation embodies compensation on the loss of the loan's purchasing power, which is not a cost item but rather a principal repayment. The periodic repayment of the inflation-compensation causes accelerated repayment of the loan. The appreciation of the asset financed by the loan, on the other hand, is only partially realized in each period through the returns covering current cost depreciation. The difference between the accelerated loan repayment and the nonrealized appreciation of the asset must be financed by interim funds, usually by short-term loans, assuming that the profit from the investment is not used for financing these needs.

In other words, given that an investment in an asset is fully financed by debt, throughout its life, the difference between recorded net asset value (historical value) and current net asset value (revalued asset) is financed by short-term loans even though the investment was originally financed by a long-term loan matched to the asset's lifespan. (For a detailed example, see section 5.3.)

Consider the example in table 1.2, where the investment is fully financed by a two-year loan, matching the investment terms. At the end of the first year, the historical value of the net asset is $50 and the current value is $60; hence, the balance sheet will show liability of $60 of which $50 is the outstanding balance of the original loan and $10 short-term loans, taken at the end of the first year.

Income tax is levied on income after allowance for historical depreciation and actual interest expense. Historical depreciation is understated, causing the well-known phenomenon of equity erosion. Interest, on the other hand, includes an inflation-compensation factor which provides a tax benefit. The difference between the equity erosion and the loan tax benefit yields the net tax benefit of the loan under conditions of inflation and with existing tax rules. In chapter 7, it is shown that this net tax benefit of a loan is always positive. Therefore, in order that taxation be neutral to inflation, the net benefit must be zero. In other words, the tax benefit from the loan must offset equity erosion. To achieve this objective, the firm must finance part of its investments by loans. In chapter 7, the break-even financial leverage is shown to be equal to the present value of historical depreciation discounted at the nominal cost of capital, divided by the invested sum.

NOTES

1. This chapter is based on Shashua and Goldschmidt (1985).

2. In order to isolate the pure effect of inflation on cash flow and to simplify the presentation, it is assumed that inflation is neutral on all prices, is uniform, and is fully anticipated. The unanticipated effect, the end result of which is an increase in uncertainty, is not analyzed here.

3. Many pitfalls can be found in the economic and accounting literature regarding this point. For example, the Financial Accounting Standards Board (1979) classifies inventories together with property, plant, and equipment as nonmonetary assets in their Statement No. 33 for financial reporting under changing prices (p. 102).

4. The loan service per period is $a_{n,h}^{-1}$ and the cash inflow at period t is $E_t = a_{n,r}^{-1} (1+p)^t$, where $a_{n,x}^{-1}$ is the capital recovery at discounting rate x.

5. A proof for a depreciable fixed asset under the discrete case is given in Shashua and Goldschmidt (1984).

6. The practice of charging depreciation and materials drawn from inventories at current replacement values in conjunction with market interest rates on current asset values can be inferred from statements by business leaders (e.g., Bailey, 1978; Symonds, 1982) and is used in preparing production and cost budgets (e.g., U.S. Department of Agriculture, 1981b). The logic of this practice is that the firm should recover the current replacement costs, which is the same as the condition of avoiding nonnegative cash flow in each period.

7. The application of the Financial Accounting Standards Board Statement No. 33 (FASB, 1979), which applies to large public enterprises in the United States, causes such a bias. Under FASB procedure, both depreciation and cost of materials drawn from inventories are adjusted. Therefore, the "income from continuing operation" is understated in leveraged firms, as shown by Goldschmidt and Shashua (1984).

8. Feldstein and Summers (1978) analyzed, in empirical research, the effect of inflation, taxation and leverage on the market interest rates.

PART ONE

THE BEHAVIOR OF WORKING CAPITAL DURING INFLATION

TWO

WORKING CAPITAL FOR A PRODUCTION PROCESS

Interest expenses on working capital are a relatively insignificant factor in budgeting and costing agricultural crops and enterprises as long as interest rates are low. However, when interest is high, the cost of working capital for prolonged agricultural production processes becomes a significant item. For example, when the interest rate is 20 percent per annum, the cost of working capital for cotton in Arizona is estimated to be 7.5 percent of the revenue.

During inflation, the market interest rates embody a premium for maintaining the purchasing power of the loan's principal, which is, as a matter of fact, principal repayment rather than a cost item. For example, a 10 percent inflation rate that causes interest rates to rise from 5 percent to 15 percent would cause interest expenses to treble, whereas the cost of other goods will rise by approximately 10 percent. Therefore, during inflation the interest expense rises by more than the inflation factor, in contrast to the behavior of other cost items in the production process.

Another way inflation affects operating costs is the so-called "efficiency illusion" in relating costs to gross income. Costs (excluding interest) which are usually expended during the production process are often related to gross income at the end of the process when the price level is higher. Thus, the higher the price level rises during the production process, the lower the ratio of costs to gross income. This inflation-induced lower ratio is complemented by an inflation-induced higher ratio of interest on working capital to gross income.

The need for working capital for a crop is derived from a cash flow budget for a full cycle of the production process. In order to compare the need for working capital of various production processes, some measures are proposed and applied in this chapter. To illustrate the sensitivity of interest on working capital with respect to inflation, the proposed procedures are applied to cost budgets of two agricultural enterprises in Arizona.

2.1 NEEDS AND MEASURES FOR WORKING CAPITAL

Working capital is defined here as the capital required for financing the current operations of a production process up to the time when receipts from output are received. The periodic and total needs for working capital are determined by (1) the nature of the production process (duration, seasonality, level of required inventories, and so on), (2) by the practices of payments for inputs and outputs, and (3) by the respective rates of inflation and interest.

A simplified example is used to illustrate the need for working capital, assuming that all the transactions are made in cash. Consider the quarterly cash flow for one acre of Crop A and one acre of Crop B, as presented in table 2.1. The finance need (payments less interim receipts), which represent the need for working capital, is assumed to be financed by equity funds.

The resulting quarterly needs for working capital, as presented in table 2.1, provide the schedule of finance that the grower must ascertain for each planned acre. The cumulative need will be repaid by the realized receipts at the end of the production cycle.

To compare the needs for working capital of different crops, three measures are proposed, each providing some comparable information. The first measure, "total needs for working capital," is expressed as "dollars × periods" and indicates the volume of finance that the grower has to allocate to the crop. For example, the needs for an acre of Crop A are 900 "dollars × quarters" whereas the corresponding needs of Crop B are only 450 "dollars × quarters."[1] The second measure, "working capital to costs," is the ratio of total needs to total payments (variable costs in the example). This ratio indicates the amount of working capital, in "dollars × periods" terms, required for each dollar of the relevant costs. Thus, the need of Crop A and Crop B is, respectively, 2.25 and 1.50 "dollars × quarters" for each dollar of variable cost. The third measure, "average working capital," is the total need for working capital divided by the number of periods that the capital is needed ($225 per quarter for each crop).

As Crop A has a longer production cycle than Crop B, it requires more working capital. The greater needs are indicated by two measures,

Table 2.1 Cash Flow and Working Capital under Equity Finance (per acre)

	Jan. 1	March 31	June 30	Sept. 30	Dec. 31	Total
Crop A						
Payments (variable costs)	$100	$100	$100	$100	$—	$ 400
Receipts (revenue)			(50)		(750)	(800)
Cash requirements	100	100	50	100		350
Finance needs	100	200	250	350	—	
Net receipts						(400)
Measures:						
Total needs for working capital						$×Q 900[a]
Working capital to costs[b]						2.25
Average working capital[c]						$ 225
Crop B						
Payments (variable costs)		$150	$150	$ —		$ 300
Receipts (revenue)				(500)		(500)
Cash requirements		150	150			300
Finance needs		150	300			
Net receipts						(200)
Measures:						
Total needs for working capital						$×Q 450[a]
Working capital to costs[b]						1.50
Average working capital[c]						$ 225

[a]Summation of the row, indicating volume of working capital in "dollars × quarters" terms.
[b]Total needs to total payments; indicating volume of "dollars × quarters" per dollar of cost.
[c]Total needs divided by four quarters, indicating dollars per quarter.
Note: Figures in parentheses represent inflow.

total needs per acre and relative needs per dollar of outlay. The average needs per quarter are, however, equal for both crops.

Aggregate Needs for Working Capital

The requirements for working capital per acre of an individual crop, as presented in table 2.1, provide the building blocks for determining aggregate needs or demand for financing working capital for a firm or region. The aggregation can be calculated for various purposes of financial planning.

Aggregation is carried out by adding the periodic needs for working capital of the individual crops. The items to be grouped together differ depending on whether a region or a farm is considered. In the case of aggregation at the region level, the surplus of receipts over the cumulative payments at the end of the production cycle of each crop should not be taken into account. The cash surplus should be viewed as the growers' disposable income. The need for working capital can be viewed as the demand for financing; this demand is supplied, at both region and farm levels, by equity funds or loans, and at the farm level, additionally by the surplus generated by other crops. At the farm level, the additional need for investments should be added to the aggregate demand in determining the cash flow budget.[2]

2.2 COST OF WORKING CAPITAL

Working capital requirements of a crop can be financed by either equity funds or loans. In both cases there are related costs, but with loans, it is easier to illustrate the cost through interest expenses. Consider again Crop A and Crop B, and suppose working capital is financed by a line of credit. The periodic needs for working capital, including the interest charges, are presented by the periodic outstanding loan balances in table 2.2.

The figures in table 2.2 show that periodic loan balances are higher than the respective needs for working capital under equity finance by the amount of the interest expenses. The cumulative loan balance, which equals the demand for working capital ($377.87 and $313.64 per acre, for Crops A and B respectively) are repaid at the end of production cycle from receipts.

In the two illustrative crops, receipts occur at the end of the production process (except for an interim receipt for Crop A). Under this scheme of cash flow, total interest expenses indicates the real cost of working capital. Net income is, therefore, stated in real terms for the date of its realization (December 31 for Crop A; September 30 for Crop B). For comparing the profitability of different crops, the net income figures must be discounted to a base date. If the scheme of cash flow of a crop differs from that of the two examples cited here—for instance if payments follow the receipts—then the real cost of working capital should be determined by discounting the periodic payments. Since such a cash flow scheme is not typical to most agricultural enterprises, it is not discussed here.

The figures in table 2.2 show that because the production cycle of Crop A is longer than that of Crop B, the corresponding total interest expenses per acre are higher ($27.87 compared to $13.64). If one wishes to compare the cost of working capital of different crops,

Table 2.2   Cash Flow and Operating Capital under Debt Finance (per acre)

	Jan. 1	March 31	June 30	Sept. 30	Dec. 31	Total
Crop A						
Payments (variable costs)	$100.00	$100.00	$100.00	$100.00	$ —	$400.00
Receipts (revenue)			(50.00)		(750.00)	(800.00)
Cash requirements	100.00	100.00	50.00	100.00		350.00
Finance needs	100.00	200.00	250.00	350.00	—	
Interest, 3%, quarterly[a]		3.00	6.09	7.77	11.01	27.87
Loan balance[b]	100.00	203.00	259.09	366.86	377.87	
Net receipts						(372.13)
Measures:						
Total needs for working capital						$×Q 928.95[c]
Interest to variable costs						6.97%
Interest to revenue						3.48
Crop B						
Payments (variable costs)		$150.00	$150.00	$ —		$300.00
Receipts (revenue)				(500.00)		(500.00)
Cash requirements		150.00	150.00			
Interest, 3%, quarterly[a]			4.50	9.14		13.64
Loan balance[b]		150.00	304.50	313.64		
Net receipts						(186.36)
Measures:						
Total needs for working capital						$×Q 454.50[c]
Interest to variable costs						4.55%
Interest to revenue						2.73

[a]Interest on previous quarter's loan balance.
[b]Loan balance in previous quarter plus current quarter's cash requirement and interest.
[c]Total loan balances for four quarters prior to the loan repayment on Dec. 31. This figure indicates volume of finance in "dollars × quarters."
Note: Figures in parentheses represent inflow. The needs for working capital are financed by debt, therefore the needs are equal to the loan balances.

interest expenses can be related to either relevant costs (payments) or to revenue. The first ratio, "interest to costs," shows how much the interest on working capital inflates the costs (6.97 percent for Crop A, 4.55 percent for Crop B). The second ratio, "interest to revenue," shows the share of interest on working capital relative to total revenue (3.48 percent and 2.73 percent, respectively).

2.3 EFFECT OF INFLATION ON WORKING CAPITAL

During a period of inflation the prices of inputs, outputs, and capital all rise. As a result, the nominal volume of production costs and the

Table 2.3   Cash Flow and Working Capital during Inflation, Crop A, Debt Finance (per acre)

	Jan. 1	March 31	June 30	Sept. 30	Dec. 31	Total
Price Index	100.000	105.000	110.250	115.762	121.551	
Payments (variable costs)[a]	$100.00	$105.00	$110.25	$115.76	$ —	$431.01
Receipts (revenue)[a]			(55.13)		(911.63)	(966.76)
Cash requirements	100.00	105.00	55.12	115.76		375.88
Finace needs	100.00	205.00	260.12	375.88		
Interest, 8.15%, quarterly[b]		8.15	17.37	23.28	34.61	83.41
Loan balance[c]	100.00	213.15	285.64	424.68	459.29	
Net receipts						(452.34)
Measures:						
Total needs for working capital						$×Q 1,023.47[d]
Interest to variable costs						19.35%
Interest to revenue						8.58

[a]Figures from table 2.1 multiplied by the price index divided by 100.
[b]Inflation-compensated interest on previous quarter's loan balance.
[c]Loan balance in previous quarter plus current quarter's cash requirement and interest.
[d]Total loan balance for four quarters prior to the loan repayment on Dec. 31. This figure indicates volume of finance in "dollars × quarters."
Note: Figures in parentheses represent inflow.

nominal interest rates increase and, in turn, the need for—and cost of—working capital are forced upwards, as illustrated below.

For the sake of simplicity, assume that all prices rise by the same rate—by the inflation rate. The level of the pre-inflation outlays and receipts will rise by p per quarter, and the pre-inflation interest rate, r^*, is assumed to be fully compensated and, therefore, will rise to a nominal rate, r, as follows:

$$r = (1 + r^*)(1 + p) - 1$$

Suppose the expected inflation is 5 percent per quarter; then, the pre-inflation interest rate of 3 percent per quarter will rise to the following nominal rate:

$$r = (1 + 0.03)(1 + 0.05) - 1 = 0.0815 = 8.15\%$$

Consider the situation of Crop A under these conditions. The corresponding cash flow and need for working capital are presented in table 2.3. As the price level advance 5 percent per quarter affects all variables equally, the crop's real net income should not be changed by the inflation. In other words, the $452.34 net receipts on December

31 under inflation (table 2.3) will be equal to the $372.13 pre-inflation figure (table 2.2) multiplied by the price level increase ($372.13 × 1.21551).

The effect of inflation on working capital can be seen by analyzing the figures in table 2.4 where data and measures for Crop A, under four alternative situations, are presented. The figures in table 2.4 are presented as a comparison between constant and inflated price levels but an equally valuable comparison can be observed between equity and debt finance.

The main differences between the figures under inflation and those under constant price level are: (1) the increase in nominal interest expenses and raatios; (2) the decrease in the ratio of variable costs to revenue, causing an "efficiency illusion"; and (3) the absence of any significant change in the ratio of working capital to costs. The last indicator shows that the need for working capital, relative to the costs, is not affected by inflation. The volume of costs and the need for finance are inflated; thus, the ratio of working capital to costs is not inflated.

The ratios of interest on working capital to revenue and variable costs to revenue should be seen as complementing each other. In computing any financial ratio, both figures in the ratio should be stated at the same price level. Thus, in computing the ratio of variable costs to revenue, the corresponding cash flows must be inflation-adjusted to the end of the production cycle. It should be noted, however, that an equivalent adjustment must be carried out by the inflation fraction within the nominal interest charges for the loan that finances the cash requirements. Instead of adjusting the variable costs, we can add the nominal interest expenses to the nominal variable costs in computing a ratio of total variable costs to revenue, as follows:

Under constant price level: $\dfrac{400.00 + 27.87}{800.00} = 0.535 = 53.5\%$

Under inflation: $\dfrac{431.01 + 83.41}{966.76} = 0.532 = 53.2\%$

As can be seen, the ratios are almost equal; interim receipts cause the slight differences. Note that the nominal interest on working

Table 2.4 Data and Measures of Working Capital for Crop A (per acre)

	Variable Costs			Interest			Working Capital		
	Revenue	Total	To Revenue	Total	To Costs	To Revenue	Total Needs[a]	To Costs[b]	Average per Quarter
Constant price level									
Equity Finance (table 2.1)	$800.00	$400.00	50.0%				$×Q 900.00	$×Q 2.25	$225
Debt Finance (table 2.2)	800.00	400.00	50.0%	$27.87	6.97%	3.48%	928.95	2.32	232
Inflation (5 percent per quarter)									
Equity finance	$966.76	$431.01	44.6%				$×Q 941.00	$×Q 2.18	$235
Debt finance (table 2.3)	966.76	431.01	44.6	$83.41	19.35%	8.58%	1,023.47	2.37	256

[a] Volume of working capital in "dollars × quarters" terms.
[b] Total needs to total variable costs, indicating volume of "dollars × quarters" per dollar of variable costs.

capital complements the nominal variable costs; these two figures represent the real variable costs.

2.4 EFFECT OF INFLATION ON WORKING CAPITAL FOR TWO FARM ACTIVITIES

The effect of inflation on working capital and the interest thereon is illustrated in this section using two farm activities, a cotton and a beef herd, both with a one-year production cycle. They differ in their schemes of receipts; cotton's receipts occur at the end of the year, whereas receipts for the beef herd occur three times during the course of the year. Source of the data is USDA-ESCS production budgets for Arizona in 1979.[3]

The computations are based on monthly outlays assuming that (1) the transactions are in cash and therefore cash flow coincides with the budget's items, (2) no feed inventories are held for the beef herd, and (3) the fixed costs (except for interest on assets) are evenly distributed over the year, in constant prices, and therefore are included in the payments. Inflation-free interest on the loans which finance working capital is set at 3 percent per annum (that is, 0.2466 percent per month).

The resulting ratio of working capital to costs, assuming stable price conditions, shows that cotton's need for working capital, per dollar of total costs, is more than double that of the beef herd (4.88 versus 2.33 in "dollars × months") because of the different pattern of receipts. Interest for working capital for cotton and the beef herd, respectively, comprise 1.15 and 0.57 percent of the revenue. When the interest rate for cotton's working capital increases from 3 percent to 20 percent per annum, the ratio of interest to revenue rises from 1.15 percent to about 7.5 percent.

The effect of inflation on the working capital needed for the two activities is analyzed by applying the procedure illustrated in table 2.3 using a series of inflation rates from 0 to 50 percent. The computational procedures are illustrated and explained in the appendix to this chapter. To save space, the results are not presented except for those showing the effect of inflation on interest expenses and other costs.

The analysis in the previous section shows that inflation affects the ratios of interest to revenue and cost to revenue in opposite directions. The effect of inflation on these ratios, for the two enterprises,

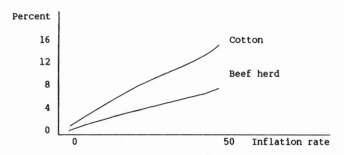

Fig. 2.1 Ratios of interest on working capital to
revenue: two farm activities in Arizona

is presented in figures 2.1 and 2.2. The curves in both figures show
that inflation radically affects the ratios for both activities. However,
the ratios for cotton are affected much more than those for the beef
herd because the former's relative need for working capital is significantly larger.

The curves in figure 2.1 show that under an inflation rate of 14
percent (approximately the actual 1979 rate in the United States), the
ratio of interest on working capital to revenue was about 6 percent
and 3 percent for cotton and the beef herd, respectively. The curves
in figure 2.2 show that the ratios of costs to revenue declined with
the increase in the inflation rate. By adding the two ratios together,
however, one arrives at a figure more or less constant for all the
inflation rates.

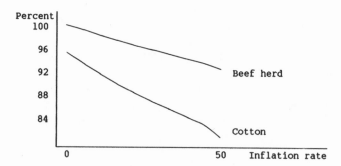

Fig. 2.2 Ratios of costs to revenue: two farm
activities in Arizona

Some Implications

During a period of inflation, the nominal needs for, and the cost of, working capital are higher than those during a period of constant prices. However, the ratio of working capital to costs is not affected by inflation. In other words, the volume of finance allocated for working capital in agriculture needs to be adjusted to changes in the price level of the inputs used in production.

Interest rates in a period of inflation embody a compensation for the expected decline in the purchasing power of the loan's principal. This causes nominal interest expenses to increase by more than the inflation rate. In turn, the ratio of interest expense to revenue increases, while the ratio of other inputs (recorded historical costs) to revenue is understated during inflation, causing an "efficiency illusion." The summation of interest expenses on working capital and other costs make it possible to compute a ratio of costs to revenue which can be used also in a period of inflation.

NOTES

1. The total needs for working capital, in "dollars $\times$ periods" terms, can be calculated by

$$\sum_{t=1}^{T} (\text{Finance needs at } t)(T - t)$$

where T = number of periods from the date of the first payment to the date when the receipts exceed the cumulative payments. For Crop A, where $T = 5$, the total needs for working capital are:

$$100(5 - 1) + 100(5 - 2) + 50(5 - 3) + 100(5 - 4) = 900$$

The resulting figure can be used for approximating the cost of working capital by multiplying this sum by the relevant rate of interest per period. Suppose the interest rate is 3 percent per quarter, then the interest charges are approximately 900×0.03 = \$27. The exact figure is calculated in table 2.2.

2. For details see, e.g., Barry, Hopkins, and Baker (1983); and Penson and Lins (1980).

3. For source and details, see the appendix to this chapter. The year 1979 was chosen because of the high inflation (almost 14 percent). The nominal figures in the production budgets have been converted into constant dollars before applying the procedures that are illustrated on the hypothetical crops in tables 2.2 and 2.3. Since the budget for the beef herd shows a loss, the fixed costs were reduced by the amount of the loss.

Table 2.A   Cash Flow for Cotton, Arizona 1979 (dollars per acre)

Month (end)	12/78	1/79	2/79	3/79	4/79	5/79
CPI	100.000	100.867	102.0774	103.1567	104.3973	105.6178
Nominal prices						
Variable costs		0.98	3.58	26.36	50.57	87.10
Fixed costs		17.63	17.84	18.03	18.25	18.46
Revenue						
Cash requirements		18.61	21.42	44.39	68.82	105.56
Constant prices						
Variable costs		0.97	3.51	25.55	48.44	82.47
Fixed costs		17.48	17.48	17.48	17.48	17.48
Revenue						
Cash requirements		18.45	20.99	43.03	65.92	99.95

Table 2.B   Cash Flow and Working Capital for Cotton, Arizona 1979 (dollars per acre)

Month (end)	12/78	1/79	2/79	3/79	4/79	5/79
Inflation index	1.00	1.015309	1.030853	1.046635	1.062659	1.078927
Variable cost		0.99	3.62	26.75	51.48	88.98
Fixed cost		17.75	18.02	18.29	18.57	18.86
Revenue						
Cash requirements		18.73	21.63	45.04	70.05	107.84
Finance needs		18.73	40.37	85.41	155.46	263.29
Loan balance		18.73	40.70	86.47	158.06	268.71
Interest, cumulative		0.00	0.33	1.06	2.60	5.41

6/79	7/79	8/79	9/79	10/79	11/79	12/79	Total
106.8787	108.0891	109.1784	110.2073	111.1756	112.1540	113.3543	
69.50	66.13	63.01	17.56	0.98	167.30	7.31	560.38
18.68	18.89	19.08	19.26	19.43	19.60	19.81	224.99
						(862.40)	(862.40)
88.18	85.02	82.09	36.82	20.41	186.90	(835.28)	(77.03)
65.03	61.18	57.71	15.93	0.88	149.17	6.45	517.29
17.48	17.48	17.48	17.48	17.48	17.48	17.48	209.76
						(760.80)	(760.80)
82.51	78.66	75.19	33.41	18.36	166.65	.(736.87)	(33.75)

(20 percent annual inflation rate, 3 percent annual real interest rate)

6/79	7/79	8/79	9/79	10/79	11/79	12/79	Total
1.095445	1.112216	1.129243	1.146531	1.164084	1.181906	1.20	
71.23	68.05	65.17	18.27	1.03	176.30	7.74	579..59
19.15	19.44	19.74	20.04	20.35	20.66	20.98	231.85
						(912.96)	(912.96)
90.38	87.49	84.91	38.31	21.37	196.96	(884.25)	(101.53)
353.67	441.16	526.07	564.38	585.76	782.72	101.53	3817.03
363.88	457.85	550.91	599.03	631.08	839.29	−30.01	4014.70
10.20	16.68	24.84	34.65	45.32	56.57	71.52	71.52

APPENDIX
COMPUTATIONS OF WORKING OPERATING CAPITAL FOR COTTON PRODUCTION UNDER INFLATION

The purpose of this appendix is to illustrate and explain the computational procedures used in evaluating the effect of inflation on working capital for two agricultural enterprises (section 2.4), using cotton as an example.

Data from "Cotton Production Budget" for Arizona, 1979, taken from the "Firm Enterprise Data System" (U.S. Department of Agriculture, 1981a), were used for computing the needs and cost of working capital under a series of assumed inflation rates (0 to 50 percent per annum).

Appendix Table 2.A

The monthly variable costs and revenue figures in nominal prices are from the production budget, the figures in parentheses representing inflow. Fixed costs are recorded in the production budget as a total in nominal prices. To allocate this total sum among months, we assumed that the payment of fixed costs is distributed evenly over the months, in constant prices. In nominal prices, each month's payment is higher than the preceding one by that month's inflation; that is, each month's payment is multiplied by $1 + P_t$, where P_t = inflation rate in month t. In other words, the nominal monthly payments of fixed costs are proportional with the Consumer Price Index (CPI).

The fixed costs in month t are derived as follows:

$$F_t = \frac{F}{S} I_t$$

where F = total fixed costs in nominal prices,
S = sum of the CPI's for the 12 months,
I_t = CPI in month t.

The cash flow figures, in constant prices, are derived from the nominal figures by dividing the month's figures by the corresponding CPI.

Appendix Table 2.B

Consider the case of inflation rate at 20 percent per annum, or 1.5309 percent per month. The monthly cash flow of costs and revenue, in nominal prices, is derived by multiplying the original figures, in constant prices (see foot of appendix table 2.A), by the inflation index. The monthly inflation compensated interest rate if

$$(\sqrt[12]{1 + 0.03} \times \sqrt[12]{1 + 0.20}) - 1 = 0.0178135$$

The cumulative working capital is derived by compounding the previous month's balance by 1.0178135 plus the current month's cash requirements. The cumulative interest figures are calculated as the difference between the loan balance and the finance needs (cumulative cash requirements).

THREE

ESTIMATING INTEREST EXPENSES ON WORKING CAPITAL OF THE FIRM

The interest on working capital for a firm plays an important role in the measurement of operating income during a period of inflation. This is because not all interest expense should be considered as a cost of production (see chapter 9). Therefore, correct estimate of interest on working capital plays a crucial part in analyzing financial activities under conditions of inflation.

The interest on a firm's working capital cannot be estimated by aggregating the needs for the firm's various production processes, as defined in the preceding chapter. The reasons are: (1) the accounting period does not coincide with the production cycles of the individual processes, and (2) the cash surplus of one process can be used to finance the needs for working capital of other processes. Hence the level of interest on working capital should be estimated from the firm's cash flow.

In this chapter, the principles underlying the estimation of working capital are explained. Besides the cash flow method, we developed procedures for estimating the interest on working capital from financial statements data.

3.1 DETERMINING INTEREST EXPENSES FROM CASH FLOW

Interest expenses on working capital for a firm can best be determined from cash flow figures. Such a procedure is illustrated with a simplified example, assuming first, constant prices (in this section) and later on, inflationary conditions (in the next section). The example is based

Table 3.1   Cash Flow under Stable Production, Constant Prices

	Carried from Last Year	Quarters				Carried to Next Year	Total
		1	2	3	4		
Payments		$200	$200	$200	$200		$800
Inventories	$200					$200	
Receipts		(250)	(250)	(250)	(250)		(1,000)
Receivables	250					250	
Current assets	450					450	
Cash requirements[a]		(50)	(50)	(50)	(50)		
Finance needs[b]	450	400	350	300	250	250	

[a]Receipts minus payments.
[b]Cumulative.
Note: Figures in parentheses represent inflow.

on the following assumptions: (1) payments on inputs are made upon acquisition; (2) materials are held in inventory for one quarter and the FIFO (first in first out) accounting method is used; (3) receipts on sales are received one quarter after actual invoicing—that is, the firm provides its customers with credit for one quarter without interest. However, under inflation (section 3.2) interest is charged on this credit.

Consider first a case of a stable level of production. The corresponding quarterly cash flow, stated in constant prices for the date of the opening balance sheet, is presented in table 3.1. During the year, the firm sells goods for $1,000 and acquires inputs for $800; thus, the residue to equity and interest on working capital is $200. Current assets at the beginning of the year ($200 inventories and $250 receivables) are financed by short-term loans. During the year, there is a cash surplus of $50 per quarter, which is used for reducing finance needs (from $450 at the beginning of the year to $250 at the end of the year). In other words, both the residue to equity and the surplus of cash receipts are 20 percent of sales.

Consider now a case where the level of production is growing in real terms—the sales grow by $12.5 each quarter and the costs by $10 each quarter. The corresponding production schedule and cash flow are presented in table 3.2. The total value of production is $1,125 and total costs before interest on working capital are $900, thus the residue to equity before interest on working capital is $225. These figures are 12.5 percent higher than under conditions of stable

Table 3.2 Cash Flow under Growing Production, Constant Prices

	Carried from Last Year	Quarters				Carried to Next Year	Total
		1	2	3	4		
Production	$	$262.50	$275.00	$287.50	$300.00	$	$1,125.00
Costs		210.00	220.00	230.00	240.00		900.00
Cash flow							
Payments		210.00	220.00	230.00	240.00		900.00
Inventories	200.00					240.00	
Receipts		(250.00)	(262.50)	(275.00)	(287.50)		(1,075.00)
Receivables	250.00					300.00	
Current assets	450.00					540.00	
Cash requirements		(40.00)	(42.50)	(45.00)	(47.50)		(175.00)
Finance needs	450.00	410.00	367.50	322.50	275.00	275.00	
Interest, 1% quarterly[a]		4.50	4.15	3.76	3.35		15.76
Loan balance[b]	450.00	414.50	376.14	334.91	290.76	290.76	
Cash Residue[c]							(159.24)

[a]Interest on previous quarter's loan balance.
[b]Loan balance in previous quarter plus current quarter's cash requirement and interest.
[c]Receipts minus payments and interest.
Note: Figures in parentheses represent inflow.

production (table 3.1). The accounting income statement provides a different picture, as follows:

Sales		$1075
Cost of goods sold: Opening inventories	$200	
Purchases	900	
Closing inventories	(240)	
		860
Net income before interest on working capital		215

These figures are 7.5 percent higher than under the conditions of stable production. Current assets increased from $450 to $540—that is, by 20 percent—and cash surplus reduced finance needs by $175 (from $450 to $275). These figures show that when there is growth in the volume of production, the needs for working capital increase by a larger percentage. This is because growth implies investment in current assets.

Table 3.3 Cash Flow under Growing Production and Inflation

	Carried from Last Year	Quarters 1	2	3	4	Carried to Next Year	Total
Price index		105.000	110.250	115.763	121.551		
Production[a]	$	$275.60	$303.20	$332.80	$364.70	$	$1,276.30
Costs[a]		220.50	242.60	266.20	291.70		1,021.00
Cash flow							
Payments		220.50	242.60	266.20	291.70		1,021.00
Inventories	200.00					291.70	
Receipts[b]		(265.00)	(292.10)	(321.40)	(352.80)		(1,231.30)
Receivables	250.00					364.70	
Current assets	450.00					656.40	
Cash requirements		(44.50)	(49.50)	(55.20)	(61.10)		(210.30)
Finance needs	450.00	405.50	356.00	300.80	239.70	239.70	
Interest, 6% quarterly[c]		27.00	26.00	24.50	22.70		100.20
Loan balance[d]	450.00	432.50	409.00	378.30	339.90	339.90	
Cash Residue[e]							(110.10)

[a]Figures in table 3.2 multiplied by the price index and dividend by 100.
[b]Production in previous quarter plus 6 percent interest.
[c]Interest on previous quarter's loan balance.
[d]Loan balance in previous quarter plus current quarter's cash requirement and interest.
[e]Receipts minus payments and interest.
Note: Figures in parentheses represent inflow.

Suppose finance needs are met by loans at 1 percent interest per quarter, computed on the opening balance of each quarter, as shown at the bottom of table 3.2. The total interest expense is $15.76 which comprises only 1.47 percent of the sales. In comparison, total interest under zero growth condition is computed to be $13.86. The total finance needs increased by the amount of interest and are financed by the loan. Thus, the loan balances each quarter represent the total needs for working capital.

3.2 DETERMINING INTEREST EXPENSES UNDER INFLATION

Consider inflationary conditions where all the prices rise by 5 percent per quarter. Thus, the quarterly production and cost figures under constant prices (table 3.2) are inflated by the quarterly price index, as presented in table 3.3. For example, the $262.50 production in the first quarter under constant prices (table 3.2) is inflated by 1.05 (105/100) to become $275.60 in table 3.3.

Since receipts on sales are received one quarter after invoicing, interest at 6 percent per quarter is charged on the credit to customers. Thus, quarterly sales under constant prices (where interest on this credit is not charged) are inflated by the quarterly interest rate to arrive at the flow of receipts as presented in table 3.3. In other words, each receipt figure is equal to the value of production of the preceding quarter plus 6 percent interest. For example, the $275.60 production in the first quarter plus 6 percent interest provides $292.10 receipts in the second quarter.

A comparison of the figures in table 3.3 with those in table 3.2 sheds light on the effect of inflation on various aspects of working capital. First, inflation does not necessarily change the physical nature of production, but it does change the relationship of the figures derived from the accounting records. In the example, the ratio of inputs consumed, for each quarter, is 80 percent of the value of production under both inflation and no inflation. But the ratio of the recorded costs of goods sold to sales is affected by inflation, causing a so-called "efficiency illusion" in relating costs to gross income. The cost of goods sold is computed as follows:

	No Inflation	Inflation
Opening inventories	$ 200.00	$ 200.00
Purchases (costs)	900.00	1,021.00
Closing inventories	(240.00)	(291.70)
	860.00	929.30

The ratio of cost of goods sold to sales (receipts) under inflation is 75.5 percent ($929.30 to $1,231.30), compared to 80 percent under no inflation ($860.00 to $1,075.00). Viewed alternatively, inflation caused the cost of goods sold to rise by 8 percent (from $860.00 to $929.30), whereas sales figures rose by 14.5 percent (from $1,075.00 to $1,231.30).

Second, under inflation, the cash residue from operations shrinks. This is because the nominal investment in current assets under inflation is higher than under no inflation. Thus, a 5 percent inflation per quarter necessitated a $206.40 ($656.40−$450.00) investment as against a $90.00 ($540.00−$450.00) investment under growth alone, and no investment under zero growth.

Third, the interest expense on working capital rises considerably. In the example, interest rose from 1.47 percent of sales under no inflation ($15.76 interest) to 8.14 percent of sales under inflation ($100.20 interst). Thus, a 5 percent inflation per quarter caused the relative interest on working capital to rise by a factor of about 5.5 times, and absolute interest expenses to rise by about 6.4 times!

Fourth, nominal interest expenses on working capital should be added to the cost of goods sold in evaluating the performance of a firm. The relevant figures for the example are:

	No Inflation	Inflation
Cost of goods sold	$ 860.00	$ 929.30
Interest on working capital	15.76	100.20
Total costs	875.76	1,029.50
Sales	1,075.00	1,231.30
Costs to sales	81.47%	83.61%

The reason that the ratio of costs to sales under inflation is not equal to that under no inflation is that, because of the growth of production, the cost of goods sold includes some costs that will be realized in the next year. If zero growth is assumed, the corresponding ratio of costs to sales is 81.39 percent under both stable and inflation conditions.

Estimating Interest from Last Year's Data

In a period of inflation it is important to estimate interest expense on working capital because it becomes a significant cost item. On the other hand, the preparation of the cash flow figures during inflation requires tedious work and involves many uncertain factors. Therefore, a short-cut method for estimating the interest on working capital may be useful in practice. Given that the interest on working capital has been determined in the last year, interest expense in the next year can be estimated by

$$I_{C,t} = I_{C,t-1} \left(\frac{SALES_t}{SALES_{t-1}} \right) \frac{r_t}{r_{t-1}} \tag{3.1}$$

where I_C = estimated interest on working capital,
SALES = sales, nominal value,
r = interest rate, nominal,
$t, t-1$ = next and last year, respectively.

3.3 ESTIMATING INTEREST EXPENSES FROM FINANCIAL STATEMENTS

Three methods for estimating the interest on working capital from financial statement data are devised in this section. Each method is based on different assumptions and utilizes different data; thus, the user can choose the method which best suits the case under analysis.

The Pro-Rata Method

This method uses actual data, as recorded in the financial statement, in estimating the interest on working capital. Given total interest expenses on loans financing all or part of the current assets, the interest on working capital is estimated by a proportionate allocation, as follows:[1]

$$I_C = I_L \frac{W_{t-1} + W_t}{L_{t-1} + L_t} \qquad (3.2)$$

where I_C = estimated interest on working capital, that is, on W,
I_L = total interest expense on L,
W = current assets which serve as working capital, mainly inventories, receivables and cash,
L = loans financing current assets,
t, t−1 = dates of closing and opening balance sheets, respectively.

Relation (3.2) is based on the assumption that the cash surplus which is generated during the year is appropriated to dividend payments and investments. If, however, cash surplus is used to finance part of working capital, relation (3.2) should be changed. When cash surplus is used to finance working capital, it substitutes a portion of the loans, which, in turn, reduce the charge for interest. Assuming that the flow of cash surplus is evenly distributed over the year, in constant prices, relation (3.2) will take the form of

$$I_C = I_L \frac{W_{t-1} + W_t - C(s_{n,i}/n)}{L_{t-1} + L_t} \qquad (3.3)$$

where C = cash surplus as shown below,

$s_{n,i} = \dfrac{(1+i)^n - 1}{i}$ = future value or an ordinary annuity,

i = periodic (monthly) interest rate on short-term loans,
n = periods in a year (months),

$C(s_{n,i}/n)$ = cash surplus plus earnings thereon.

Cash surplus can be estimated as follows:

$$C = \text{Sales} \simeq \text{COGS} - I_F - \text{IN} \qquad (3.4)$$

where COGS = Purchases + INVY_{t-1} − INVY_t
    = cost of goods sold exclusive of depreciation,
  INVY = inventories at replacement value,
   I_F = interest expenses on loans financing fixed assets,
   IN = investment for replacing the existing assets, which can be estimated by the depreciation charges at replacement cost.

The multiplier of the cash surplus can be estimated as follows, when n = 12 and for moderate interest rates:

$$s_{n,i}/n \simeq \sqrt{1 + r} \simeq 1 + r/2 \qquad (3.5)$$

where r = annual interest rate on short-term loans

If cash surplus is not evenly distributed, and there is information on the pattern of the actual flow of cash surplus, the multiplier of C in relation (3.5) should be adjusted accordingly.

Consider the example in table 3.3. Suppose the opening balance of short term loans is $850 of which $450 finance current assets, and interest expense on these loans is $185.[2] Given that for n = 4, i = 0.06, $s_{n,i}$ = 4.374616, the interest on working capital is estimated at

$$I_C = 185 \times \frac{656.40 + 450.00 - 210.30\,(4.374616/4)}{850.00 + 739.90} = \$101.98$$

In comparison, actual interest expense calculated from the cash flow is $100.20.

The Current Assets Method

This method computes interest expenses on working capital in the same way as on cash flow figures. Interest is charged on the opening balance of the current assets, assuming that these assets are financed by loans. The periodic cash surplus reduces (or the cash deficit increases) the balance of the loans; accordingly, interest expense decreases (or increases) by the interest earned on this surplus. An important aspect of this method is the assumption of uniform distribution of the flow of cash surplus, in constant prices. The interest on working capital is estimated by

$$I_C = rW_{t-1} - C[(s_{n,i}/n) - 1] \qquad (3.6)$$

where $C[(s_{n,i}/n) - 1]$ = earnings on cash surplus.

Using the data in the example, and given that $i = 0.06$, then

$$r = (1 + 0.06)^4 - 1 = 0.262497.$$

The interest on working capital is estimated at

$$I_C = 0.262497 \times 450 - 210.3\ [(4.374616/4) - 1] = \$98.48$$

The Fund Method

This method views the stock of current assets as a fund, where additions or withdrawals are assumed to take place evenly, in constant prices, over the year. Assuming that the cash surplus is appropriated to dividend payments and investments, then, according, to relation (3.17) in the appendix to this chapter, the interest on working capital is

$$I_C = (W_t - W_{t-1}) + (W_{t-1}\ \sqrt{H}) - (W_t/\ \sqrt{H}) \qquad (3.7)$$

where $H = 1 + r$.

If cash surplus is used to finance working capital, the interest on working capital is

$$I_C = (W_t - W_{t-1}) + (W_{t-1}\ \sqrt{H}) - (W_t/\ \sqrt{H}) \\ - C\ [s_{n,i}/n) - 1] \qquad (3.8)$$

Using the data in the example, and given that $H = 1 + 0.262477$, the interest on the working capital is estimated at

$$I_C = (656.40 - 450.00) + 450\ \sqrt{1.262477} - 654.4/\sqrt{1.262477} \\ - 210.30\ [(4.374616/4) - 1] = \$108.10$$

This figure is somewhat higher than the actual interest (\$100.20) calculated from the cash flow.

The Case of Equity Financing Working Capital

The three methods, as formulated above, provide an estimate of the actual interest on working capital in the case where current assets are financed by loans. When current assets are financed partially by equity funds, however, there are two ways to determine interest expense. First, only actual interest expense on the loans financing current assets can be provided. For this purpose, the term W in all the relations should represent the portion of current assets that is financed by loans. Second, imputed interest on working capital is computed by applying the relations without any adjustment. In this case, interest expenses include actual interest on the loans and imputed interest on equity (at the loans' average rate).

Some Limitations of the Methods

In the first method, the total interest paid on loans must be known. In some cases, interest on receivables is deducted from the interest bill rather than added to sales. If this is done, the method yields incorrect results. In the second method, the interest rate must be known. If the rate is not known, it can be approximated by using relation (3.15) which appears in the chapter appendix. In the third method, the interest rate can be approximated by the inflation-compensated interest rate (real rate plus inflation rate). As the interest rate in the last two methods is stated explicitly, it can be used for analyzing the effect of a change in the interest rate on the total interest expense on working capital.

There is a common assumption underlying the three methods—that the flow of cash surplus is evenly distributed over the year, in constant prices. Thus, the total interest on this flow is estimated by the variable $C[(s_{n,i}/n) - 1]$, or approximated by $C[\sqrt{H-1}]$, or by $C(r/2)$. When this assumption does not hold and there is information on the pattern of the flow of the cash surplus, the interest on this flow should be estimated accordingly.

3.4 ANALYTICAL RELATIONSHIP BETWEEN INFLATION AND INTEREST EXPENSES

The current asset method for estimating interest on working capital (relation 3.6) is used in this section to illustrate the effect of inflation on interest expenses. The approximation of relation (3.6) is

$$I_C = r\, W_{t-1} - C\, (\sqrt{H} - 1) \tag{3.9}$$

where r = annual interest rate, nominal,

W_{t-1} = current assets, opening balance,

C = cash surplus before interest expenses on loans financing current assets

$H = 1 + r.$

The assumptions behind this relation are that the distribution of both sales and cash surplus over the year is uniform, in constant prices, and that the inflation rate is uniform.

As the level of working capital is related to the level of sales, we use the ratio of interest on working capital to sales instead of the absolute amount of interest; that is,

$$\bar{I}_C = r\,\overline{W}_{t-1} - \overline{C}\,(\sqrt{H}-1) \tag{3.10}$$

where $\bar{I}_C = I_C/\text{sales}$,
$\overline{W}_{t-1} = W_{t-1}/\text{sales}$,
$\overline{C} = C/\text{sales} = \text{cash surplus per \$1 of sales}$.

relation (3.10) presents interest on working capital per \$1 of sales. As the value of sales is usually known, the ratio of interest to sales provides a useful tool in various analyses.

According to Fisher's proposition,

$$r = r^*\,(1 + p) + p = r^*\,F + p \tag{3.11}$$

where r = nominal interest rate, per annum,
r^* = pre-inflation or inflation-free interest rate, per annum,
p = inflation rate, per annum,
$F = 1 + p$.

That is, the nominal rate of interest is the inflation-compensated rate.

To simplify the presentation and because the pre-inflation rate of interest is relatively small, we assume that the cash surplus earns only the inflation rate. Following this assumption and using relation (3.11), relation (3.10) will take the form of

$$\bar{I}_C = r^*\,F\,\overline{W}_{t-1} + p\,\overline{W}_{t-1} - \overline{C}\,(\sqrt{F} - 1) \tag{3.12}$$

The first term in relation (3.12) represents the real interest on current assets, the second term represents inflation-compensation on current assets, the third term represents the internal funds.

Approximating the term $\sqrt{F}-1$ by $p/2$, and assuming that $\overline{C}$ remains constant, the marginal effect of inflation on the interest on working capital is

$$d\bar{I}_C/dp = (1 + r^*)\,\overline{W}_{t-1} - \overline{C}/2 \tag{3.13}$$
$$\Delta\bar{I}_C = (d\bar{I}_C/dp)\Delta p \tag{3.14}$$

Using the data in the example (table 3.3),
$\overline{W}_{t-1} = 450.00/1231.30 = 0.36547$
$\overline{C} = 210.30/1231.30 = 0.1708,$

$$r^* = 0.04,$$
$$F = (1 + 0.05)^4 = 1.2155, \sqrt{F} - 1 = 0.1025, \text{ then,}$$
$$\overline{I_C} = (0.04 \times 1.2155 \times 0.36547) + (0.2155 \times 0.36547)$$
$$- (0.1708 \times 0.1025)$$
$$= 0.07902 = 7.9\%.$$

In comparison, the actual ratio of interest to sales, as calculated from the cash flow is 8.1 percent (100.20/1,231.30).

The marginal effect of inflation on relative interest, passing, say from 21.5 percent to 22.5 percent inflation ($\Delta P = 0.01$), using relation (3.14), is

$$\overline{\Delta I_C} = [(1 + 0.04) \, 0.36547 - 0.1708/2] \, 0.01 = 0.00295$$
$$= 0.295\%$$

The ratio of interest to sales would increase from 7.9 percent to 8.195 percent. (The exact figure, using $p = 0.225$, is 8.205%). The total increment on interest is

$$\text{Sales} \times \overline{\Delta I_C} = 1231.30 \times 0.00295 = \$3.63$$

Relation (3.14) assumes that changing the inflation rate would have no effect on the cash surplus ratio. This may be true for small changes in the inflation rate, but for large changes, inflation reduces the cash surplus ratio, as shown in section 3.2. Thus, the effect of inflation on interest on working capital is higher than estimated through relation (3.14).

APPENDIX
DERIVING THE AVERAGE INTEREST RATE
ON LOANS AND ASSETS

The effective rate of interest is usually determined by assuming that the principal remains constant throughout the year and that the interest earned is paid at the end of the year. These assumptions do not hold for a firm's stock of loans and other types of funds, where principal increments and decrements and interest payments (or earnings in the case of a fund) take place many times throughout the year.

Methods for deriving the effective interest rate under these conditions are devised in this appendix for both simple and compound interest charges under both constant and changing price levels. These methods are applicable to any type of fund, assuming that additions and withdrawals are evenly distributed over the year and that interest expenses can be considered as withdrawals or additions, as the case may be. Furthermore, the interest rate can be viewed as a growth rate of the stock (principal); thus, the methods devised in this appendix are also applicable to any growing stock—such as inventories and accounts receivable—which grow uniformly.

Let L = balance of stock of loans,
  t, t−1 = end of year and beginning of year, respectively,
  I = total interest expense on L,

r = effective annual rate of interest.

Simple Interest Charges

Given L_{t-1}, L_t, and I, the simple interest rate is calculated by Kellison (1970, p. 163).

$$r = \frac{I}{(L_{t-1} + L_t - I)/2} = \frac{2I}{L_{t-1} + L_t - I} \tag{3.15}$$

where $L_{t-1} + L_t - I$ is the average amount that earns interest.
     Given L_{t-1}, L_t and r, the total interest expense is

$$I = \frac{r(L_{t-1} + L_t)}{2 + r} \tag{3.16}$$

Compound Interest Charges

The total interest at the end of the year comprises the following two elements:
1) Interest on the opening balance, which is

$$r\, L_{t-1} = (H - 1)\, L_{t-1}$$

where $H = 1 + r$.

2) Interest on net additions during the year including the interest thereon, which is

$$L_t - H\, L_{t-1}.$$

This amount, excluding interest, calculated at the middle of the year is[3]

$$(L_t - L_{t-1})\sqrt{H}.$$

The interest on the net additions is then

$$(L_t - H\, L_{t-1}) - (L_t - H\, L_{t-1})\sqrt{H} = (L_t - H\, L_{t-1})\,(\sqrt{H} - 1)\sqrt{H}$$

The total interest, I, is the sum of (1) and (2); that is,

$$\begin{aligned} Ij &= L_{t-1}\,(H - 1) + (L_t - H\, L_{t-1})\,(\sqrt{H} - 1)/\sqrt{H} = \\ I &= L_t - L_{t-1} + \sqrt{H}\, L_{t-1} - L_t/\sqrt{H} \end{aligned} \tag{3.17}$$

The above is equivalent to[4]

$$I = r\, L_{t-1} + (\sqrt{H} - 1)\, \Delta L \tag{3.18}$$

where $\Delta L = L_t/\sqrt{H} - L_{t-1}\sqrt{H}$
          = real change between the closing and opening balances, stated at mid-year prices.

Approximating the mid-year interest rate by

$$\sqrt{H} - 1 \simeq r/2$$

then, relation (3.18) will take the form of

$$I = r\, L_{t-1} + r\, \Delta L/2 \tag{3.19}$$

Comparison between the Simple and Compound Schemes

Using the approximated mid-year interest rate throughout all the terms in relation (3.17) will provide a result that is equal to relation (3.16).[5] It should be noted that

$$r/2 \geq \sqrt{H} - 1$$

Hence, relation (3.14), which assumes simple interest, usually yields higher estimates of the interest expense, I, than that in relations (3.17), (3.18), and (3.19), given equal annual effective rates of interest, r. If, on the other hand, the exact mid-year rate derived from $\sqrt{H} - 1$ is $\bar{r}/2$, then, inserting $\bar{r}/2$ instead of $\sqrt{H} - 1$ in relation (3.17) we receive

$$I = \frac{(L_t - L_{t-1})\, \bar{r} + 2rL_{t-1}}{2 + \bar{r}} \tag{3.20}$$

For example, if r = 10%, then

$$\sqrt{1 + r} - 1 = 0.0488 = \bar{r}/2$$
$$\bar{r} = 0.0976 = 9.76\%.$$

Using the rate 9.76 percent in relation (3.20), the exact amount of interest is determined, assuming compounding interest throughout the year.

The Case of Inflation

Under inflation, additions and withdrawals are assumed to be evenly distributed in constant prices, so that the nominal additions increase by the inflation rate. In this case, relation (3.17) provides an adequate estimate of the annual nominal interest expense.[6]

NOTES

1. Given L, W, and I, then the interest on working capital is

$$I_C = I\, \frac{W_{t-1} + W_t}{L_{t-1} + L_t} \tag{a}$$

Relation (3.16) is

$$I = \frac{r(L_{t-1} + L_t)}{2 + r} \tag{b}$$

Using r, the interest charges on working capital are

$$I_C = \frac{r(W_{t-1} + W_t)}{2 + r} \tag{c}$$

Inserting (b) into (a), we get

$$I_C = \frac{r(L_{t-1} + L_t)}{2 + r} \times \frac{W_{t-1} + W_t}{L_{t-1} + L_t} = \frac{r(W_{t-1} + W_t)}{2 + r}$$

which is equal to (c).

Relation (3.2) assumes that the loans financing current assets carry the same interest rate as that on all the loans under analysis.

2. The amount of interest expenses is determined as follows: Given that the quarterly interest rate is 0.06, then

$r = (1 + 0.06)^4 - 1 = 0.262477$. Applying relation (3.16),

$$I = \frac{0.262477 \, (850.00 + 739.90)}{2 + 0.262477} = \$184.46 \simeq \$185$$

3. The net additions in a fund, assuming these are evenly distributed, behave similarly as an ordinary annuity. Hence, the amount of net additions of $L_t - H L_{t-1}$ is proportional to the future value of an ordinary annuity; that is $s_{n,i}$, whereas the sum excluding interest is proportional to n, the number of periodic additions. Thus, the sum excluding interest is

$$L_t - H \, L_{t-1}) \, n/S_{n,i}$$

It can be jproven that for $n = 12$ and moderate interest rates

$$s_{n,i}/n \simeq \sqrt{1 + I} = \sqrt{H}$$

In other words, the exact solution for determining the annual interest charges, assuming even distribution of additions, can be found by substituting the term $\sqrt{H}$ for the term $s_{n,i}/n$.

4. To prove that relation (3.18) is equal to relation (3.17), insert the value of $r = h - 1$ into relation (3.18); thus,

$$r \, L_{t-1} + (\sqrt{H} - 1) \, \Delta L = (H - 1) \, L_{t-1} + (\sqrt{H} - 1) \, (L_t/\sqrt{H}) - \sqrt{H} \, L_{t-1}$$
$$= L_t - L_{t-1} + \sqrt{H} \, L_{t-1} - L_t/\sqrt{H}$$

5. To prove that relation (3.17) is equal to relation (3.16), multiply relation (3.17) by $\sqrt{H}$; thus,

$$I \sqrt{H} = (L_t - L_{t-1}) \sqrt{H} + H \, L_{t-1} - L_t$$

using $\sqrt{H} \simeq 1 + r/2$ and $H = 1 + r$,

$$I = (1 + r/2) = (L_t - L_{t-1}) \, (1 + r/2) + L_{t-1} \, (1 + r) - L_t$$

which, after collecting terms is

$$I(1 + r/2) = \frac{L_{t-1} + L_t)r}{2} \text{ or } I = \frac{r(L_{t-1} + L_t)}{2 + r}$$

6. When the additions are increasing by the monthly inflation rate, their sum excluding interest is $s_{n,i}$ and their sum including interest is $n \, (1 + i)^{n-1}$,

where $s_{n,i} = \dfrac{(1 + i)^n - 1}{i}$

i = rate of interest per period, assumed to be equal to the periodic inflation rate,
n = number of periods (12 months).

Given that the sum including interest is

$$L_t - H\, L_{t-1}$$

the sum excluding interest is then

$$(L_t - H\, L_{t-1})\, s_{n,i}/n\, (1 + i)^{n-1} = (L_t - H\, L_{t-1})\, (1 + i)a_{n,i}/n$$

where $a_{n,i} = \dfrac{1 - (1 + i)^{-n}}{i}$

It should be noted that for $n = 12$ and moderate interest rates,

$$n/(1 + i)a_{n,i} \simeq s_{n,i}/n \simeq \sqrt{H}$$

The exact solution, in the case of inflation, assuming even distribution of additions, in constant prices, is then given by relation (3.17), by substituting the term $\sqrt{H}$ for the term $n/(1+i)a_{n,i}$.

FOUR

LEVEL AND COST OF WORKING CAPITAL IN THE UNITED STATES FARM SECTOR

Interest on working capital for the United States farm sector is estimated in this chapter using data from the financial statements and the pro-rata method described in the preceding chapter.

Interest on working capital was found to be sensitive to the nominal rate of interest and to the ratio of working capital to gross receipts. To calculate an approximate figure for interest on working capital in the United States farm sector, an empirical estimating function is provided. This function can be used as a practical tool by policymakers to assess the impact of inflation and the real interest rate on the cost of farm production.

4.1 DETERMINING THE LEVEL OF WORKING CAPITAL

Working capital at any given point in time is composed of assets that will be consumed by the production process (inventories and cash), and assets that will be realized during the accounting year (receivables). These, as well as some other assets, are all classified as current assets. In the case of the United States farm sector, current assets are composed of working capital alone, Thus the terms "current assets" and "working capital" will be used interchangeably in this discussion. The assets that are categorized as working capital for the farm sector are (1) deposits and currency, (2) crops stored,[1] and (3) livestock-in-process.

To arrive at the value of livestock-in-process, we had to estimate the share of the feeders, calves, lambs, and so on, out of the available

CASE A

Equity	Fixed assets

Real estate debt	---------------------------
---------------------------	Current assets
	(working capital)
Non-real estate debt	

CASE B

Equity	Fixed assets

Real estate debt	Current assets
---------------------------	(working capital)
Non-real estate debt	

Fig. 4.1 Schemes of balance sheets

data on the aggregate value of livestock. A rough estimate suggests that approximately one-quarter of the total stock can be considered as livestock-in-process. Thus, we used this factor to determine the level of livestock-in-process in every year under analysis.

To determine the cost of working capital, an average interest rate must be used. In the case of the United States farm sector, current assets are mainly financed by non-real estate loans. Hence, the average interest rate on these loans is used in calculating the interest charges on working capital. This rate is used also in the case where part of current assets are financed by real estate loans and equity. These two cases are depicted in figure 4.1 showing relative balances of non-real estate debt and current assets. In case A, current assets are assumed to be financed totally by non-real estate debt, a situation that prevailed in the United States farm sector during the 1970s and 1980s. In case B, on the other hand, current assets are assumed to be financed by both non-real and real estate debt and by equity, a situation that prevailed during the 1950s.

Consider some data for the United States farm sector (appendix table 10.A): In January 1983, the level of current assets was $63.1

billion, whereas the level of the non-real estate debt was $102.0 billion. In January 1950, on the other hand, the level of current assets was $17.8 billion and the total debt was $11.2 billion. In both cases, however, the average interest rate on non-real estate debt is imputed as a cost for the services of the working capital, as will be demonstrated in the next section.

4.2 CALCULATING THE INTEREST ON WORKING CAPITAL

Interest on working capital for the United States farm sector is estimated by using the pro-rata method in chapter 3. For simplifying the calculations, relations (3.3) and (3.5) are slightly modified to be

$$I_C = I_L \frac{(W_{t-1} + W_t) - C(1 + p/2)}{L_{t-1} + L_t} \qquad (4.1)$$

where I_C = interest on working capital (on current assets),
I_L = interest expense on non-real estate debt,
W = current assets,
L = non-real estate loans,
$t, t-1$ = dates of closing and opening balance sheets, respectively,
p = inflation rate,
C = cash surplus, as shown below.

Assuming that working capital finances the investments which are made during the year to replace existing assets, the cash surplus is estimated as follows:

Cash income from farming[2]
− Depreciation, as a proxy for the required investment replacing existing assets
+ Interest on non-real estate debt
= Cash surplus ≡ C

The relevant figures for the United States farm sector for 1982 (appendix tables 8.C, 10.A, and 10.F) are estimated to be

$$C = 27.92 - 19.81 + 11.35 = \$19.46 \text{ billion}$$

$$I_C = 11.35 \frac{(57.2 + 63.1) - 19.46 (1 + 0.01772)}{91.5 + 102.0} = \$5.89 \text{ billion}$$

The resulting $5.89 billion is the estimate of interest expense on working capital for the United States farm sector for 1982. In other words, out of $11.35 billion interest on non-real estate debt, $5.89 billion is attributed to loans financing current assets; the rest ($5.46 billion) is attributed to loans financing fixed assets.

Consider the data for 1950 (appendix table 10.A): current assets, $17.8 billion; non-real estate debt, $6.5 billion; and real estate debt, $4.7 billion. Thus, $5.2 billion equity is attributed to financing current assets.

Interest on working capital for 1950 (appendix tables 8.C, 10.A and 10.F) is estimated to be

$$C = 12.14 - 2.30 + 0.33 = \$10.17$$

$$I_C = 0.334 \ \frac{(17.83 + 19.18) - 10.17(1 + 0.03972)}{6.5 + 6.5} = \$0.68 \text{ billion}$$

This sum should be viewed as an imputed charge, composed of $0.33 billion interest actually paid on non-real estate debt and the balance of $0.35 billion as imputed interest on real estate debt and equity that finances current assets.

In summary, interest on working capital as estimated by relation (4.1) provides an imputed charge for the services of the current assets. The charge is based on the average interest rate on non-real estate debt, applied to average current assets. The resulting figures enable analysts to carry time series comparisons of both interest charges and operating income (chapter 10), even when financial leverage changes over the analyzed period.

4.3 TRENDS IN WORKING CAPITAL AND INTEREST ON WORKING CAPITAL

The level of working capital for the United States farm sector by items, in constant prices, for some selected years is presented in table 4.1. (Figures for each year are presented in appendix table 10.D.) The level of total working capital fluctuated during the analyzed period, 1950–1982, but there was no definite trend in its volume. The level of crops stored, which represent the major item of working capital, fluctuated considerably in the analyzed period, from a low of about $26 billion to a high of $46 billion, in January 1983 prices (appendix table 10.D). The level of deposits and currency decreased considerably from about $29 billion in 1950 to $7.8 billion in 1983, in January 1983 prices. This puzzling decline in deposits and currency may be due to inconsistent data.

Table 4.1   Level of Working Capital, U.S. Farm Sector, Selected Years (billion dollars in January 1983 prices)

	Jan. 1950	Jan. 1960	Jan. 1970	Jan. 1980	Jan. 1983	Increase 1983-1950
Deposits and currency	29.0	20.6	16.5	9.1	7.8	−21.2
Crops stored	31.5	25.6	28.1	41.9	42.1	10.6
Livestock-in-process	13.4	12.6	15.2	19.2	13.2	−0.2
Total working capital	73.9	58.8	59.8	70.2	63.1	−10.8

Source: Appendix table 10.D.

The level of interest on working capital is determined by both the level of working capital and the nominal interest rate. The interest rate on the non-real estate debt, which is used as the cost of working capital (appendix table 8.A), was more or less constant at about 5–6 percent during the period 1950–1965. But after 1966 the interest rate rose, up to about 13 percent in 1981 and 1982. This increase in the nominal interest rate caused a considerable rise in the interest expense on working capital, especially after 1979.

In order to arrive at comparable figures related to working capital, the following three ratios are computed for the United States farm sector: (1) working capital to gross receipts, (2) interest on working capital to gross receipts, and (3) interest on working capital to operating income, including the interest on working capital. The resulting ratios for the analyzed period, 1950–1982, are depicted in figure 4.2 and presented in appendix table 4.A.

The level of the current assets was more or less constant, with fluctuations over the analyzed period (table 4.1), but the value of gross receipts increased; thus, the ratio of working capital to gross receipts decreased from about 55 percent in the 1950s to about 40 percent in the 1970s and 1980s (upper graph in figure 4.2).

The level of interest charges on working capital increased concurrently with the value of gross receipts during the period 1950–1979. Interest charges were approximately 2 percent of gross receipts; but beginning with 1979, interest on working capital jumped to about 4 percent of gross receipts (middle graph in figure 4.2).

The rise in interest charges on working capital in the last decade caused this cost item to become a significant factor relative to operating income (section 10.4). Thus, the following ratio is used:

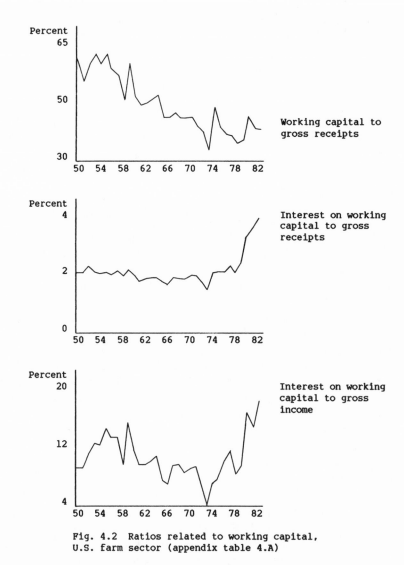

Fig. 4.2 Ratios related to working capital,
U.S. farm sector (appendix table 4.A)

$$\frac{\text{Interest on working capital}}{\text{Operating income} + \text{Interest on working capital}}$$

The resulting figures appear in the lower graph in figure 4.2. This ratio, which was about 10 percent in the 1960s and 1970s, jumped to between 15 and 20 percent in 1980–1982 (appendix table 4.A).

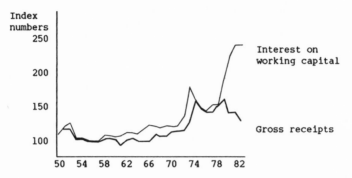

Fig. 4.3 Growth in interest on working capital,
U.S. farm sector

The relative increase of interest on working capital and of gross receipts, stated as index numbers, is presented in figure 4.3. The graphs indicate the trend, in constant prices, relative to 1950s values, which are stated as 100. As can be seen, the relative gap between interest on working capital and gross receipts increased considerably in the early 1980s.

4.4 EMPIRICAL ESTIMATION OF INTEREST ON WORKING CAPITAL

The purpose of this section is to provide an estimate of the level of interest expenses on working capital in the United States farm sector. The analytical relationship of the empirical function is delineated in section 3.4. Relation (3.10) has been used for this purpose, but the cash surplus has been disregarded for simplifying the use of the resulting function.[3]

The following regression has been estimated, using United States farm sector data for the period 1950–1982:

$$\bar{I}_C = 0.775 \; r\overline{W} \qquad (4.2)$$

where $\bar{I}_C$ = interest expense on working capital as percentage of gross receipts (second ratio in appendix table 4.a),

$\overline{W}$ = working capital, at the beginning of the year, as percentage of gross receipts (first ratio in appendix table 4.A),

r = nominal interest rate on non-real estate debt.

The adjusted r square is 0.896, the f value is 16.4, and the standard error of estimate is 0.166 percentage points relative to gross receipts.

Appendix Table 4.A   Cost and Relative Level of Working Capital, U.S. Farm Sector, 1950–1982

Year	Inflation Rate	Gross Receipts	Interest on Working Capital	Working Capital to Gross Receipts	Interest Charges to Gross Receipts	Interest Charges to Operating Income[a]
		Billion Dollars, Nominal Prices		Ratios (percent)		
1950	7.94	31.90	0.68	58.10	2.13	8.92
1951	4.20	37.00	0.81	52.91	2.19	8.96
1952	0.63	36.30	0.85	57.96	2.35	10.86
1953	1.13	32.90	0.71	60.52	2.15	12.25
1954	−0.74	32.70	0.69	57.96	2.10	12.04
1955	0.25	32.00	0.69	60.39	2.15	14.04
1956	3.11	32.50	0.67	55.78	2.06	13.06
1957	3.50	33.20	0.73	54.40	2.19	13.18
1958	1.28	37.30	0.74	47.42	1.99	9.40
1959	1.27	36.10	0.80	57.49	2.22	14.92
1960	1.59	37.10	0.76	48.09	2.04	11.37
1961	0.67	38.60	0.72	46.01	1.85	9.40
1962	1.33	40.40	0.78	46.60	1.93	9.42
1963	1.65	41.30	0.82	47.67	1.98	9.84
1964	1.08	40.10	0.79	48.83	1.97	10.62
1965	1.92	44.30	0.80	42.45	1.81	7.49
1966	3.35	48.10	0.82	42.49	1.71	6.86
1967	3.45	48.00	0.93	43.97	1.94	9.43
1968	4.61	49.20	0.94	42.42	1.91	9.51
1969	6.19	53.60	1.00	42.22	1.87	8.40
1970	5.21	55.80	1.13	42.61	2.02	9.11
1971	3.36	58.90	1.18	39.92	2.01	9.27
1972	3.65	67.70	1.21	38.09	1.79	6.57
1973	9.40	95.10	1.43	33.06	1.51	4.03
1974	11.74	93.60	1.96	44.90	2.09	7.00
1975	6.79	95.40	2.03	39.26	2.12	7.69
1976	5.16	96.90	2.08	37.74	2.14	9.91
1977	6.73	101.60	2.35	36.88	2.31	11.41
1978	9.41	119.30	2.49	35.00	2.09	8.33
1979	13.97	141.20	3.51	36.39	2.49	9.46
1980	11.74	139.40	4.64	42.65	3.33	16.50
1981	8.21	155.20	5.61	39.24	3.61	14.61
1982	3.54	149.60	5.89	38.91	3.94	18.18

[a]Interest charges on working capital divided by operating income (section 10.4) plus the interest charges on working capital.

The specific aspect of the empirical function is that interest on working capital is not determined only by the opening balance of working capital. As working capital revolves and generates cash surplus, part of the latter helps to finance the former. Therefore, interest on the working capital is not $r\overline{W}$ but rather $0.775\ r\overline{W}$. For example, if $\overline{W} = 0.40$ and $r = 0.12$, then interest on working capital is not $0.40 \times 0.12 = 0.048$, but rather 0.037. This is because only 77.5 percent of working capital bears the full burden of interest; the level of interest-bearing working capital is reduced during the year by the cash surplus.

Relation (4.2) can be used by an individual farm for arriving at a ballpark estimate of interest on working capital for costing and planning purposes. For example, suppose the ratio of working capital to sales is, on a given farm, 50 percent, and the relevant nominal interest rate is 12 percent, then

$$\overline{I}_C = 0.775 \times 0.12 \times 0.50 = 0.047$$

Given that $\overline{W}$ in the United States farm sector has been relatively constant in the last decade at about 0.40 (appendix table 4.A), then relation (4.2) can be reduced to

$$\overline{I}_C = 0.30\ r \tag{4.3}$$

This relation can be used as a rule of thumb by policymakers. For example, if the interest rate on short-term loans that are used for financing working capital is 12 percent, then interest on working capital is 3.6 percent of farm gross receipts.

When inflation does not prevail, and nominal interest is between 3 and 7 percent, interest on working capital in the United States farm sector is expected to be between 1 and 2 percent of sales, which is a negligible factor. However, when the inflation rate is on the rise, the nominal interest rate rises at a faster rate, thus causing interest on working capital to inflate and to become a significant cost item, as shown in the preceding section.

NOTES

1. Crops stored include crops held on farm under loan to CCC and crops held off farms as security for CCC loans (USDA, 1983, p. 104).

2. Cash income from farming is cash receipts from marketing and government payments less product expenses, taxes, interest, cash wages and net rent (USDA, 1983, pp. 17, 18). Operators' living expenses should be deducted from cash surplus. On the

other hand, off-farm income may be considered as financing part of the operators' living expenses. Because such detailed data are not available, both items are ignored in our analysis.

3. Disregarding cash surplus is based on the assumption that it is more or less a constant fraction of sales, in the analyzed period.

PART TWO

THE PROBLEMS OF FINANCIAL LIQUIDITY AND TAXATION DURING INFLATION

FIVE

THE BURDEN OF LOANS ON FIRMS DURING INFLATION

 Inflation has a damaging effect on investment in fixed assets, whether equity or debt are used for financing. When investment is financed by equity, inflation-induced equity erosion occurs because income tax authorities recognize only historical depreciation. When investment is financed by loans, on the other hand, inflation-induced behavior of the interest weakens the liquidity position of the firm. This chapter is devoted to analyzing the latter problem (the problem of equity erosion is discussed in chapter 7).

The specific behavior of interest during times of inflation causes an unplanned accelerated repayment of long-term loans which must then be refinanced. Since long-term loans are usually provided for financing long-term investments, the unplanned finance needs are usually supplied by short-term loans. Thus, in inflationary conditions, an investment in fixed assets that was originally financed properly by long-term loans will be, after some time, financed to some extent by short-term loans as well. Such a situation implies worsening of the liquidity position of the firm. If, however, the investment is financed by an indexed loan, inflationary conditions will not damage the liquidity position of the firm (for details see chapter 6).

The effect of inflation on the liquidity position of the firm is illustrated by an example of an investment in a fixed asset, financed fully by a loan, where the terms of both investment and loan are equal. The results demonstrated by this example hold also for a case where the investment is financed only partially by loans. For simplicity, uncertainty and income tax are ignored.

5.1 EFFECT OF INFLATION ON LOAN REPAYMENT

The process of inflation affects the nominal market rates of interest, assuming that the real, inflation-free interest rate on riskless securities remains unchanged. As early as 1930, Fisher stated that the nominal interest rate is the real interest rate plus the expected inflation rate; that is,

$$r = r^* + p \tag{5.1}$$

where r = market, nominal interest rate;

$\quad r^*$ = real, long run pre-inflation rate;

$\quad p$ = expected inflation rate;

and where r^* and p are rates in a continuous process.

In a discrete process the nominal interest rate is

$$r = (1+r^*)(1+p) - 1 = r^* + p + r^*p = $$
$$r^*(1+p) + p \tag{5.2}$$

where r is called inflation-compensated rate because it fully compensates the creditor for the decline in the purchasing power (real value) of his principal. When the inflation rate is low the value of r^*p in relation (5.2) is negligible.

To simplify the presentation, assume that the inflation is fully expected; that is, the actual inflation rate equals the expected rate. Let A be the loan's principal, then the interest on the loan, paid at the end of the period, is

$$rA = pA + r^* [(1+p)A] \tag{5.3}$$

where A = loan principal,

$\quad p$ = inflation rate.

That is, interest expense is composed of (1) inflation-compensation on the principal, and (2) real interest on the principal, in year-end prices. The inflation premium, pA, is equal to the decline in the purchasing power of the principal during the period. If this sum is added to the principal at the end of the period, the loan's real value would be intact. Therefore, pA is not a real expense item but rather can be viewed as a loan repayment item. In other words, as the variable pA is embodied in the nominal interest rate, a fraction of the loan repayment is included in interest expense. This phenomenon is illustrated below.

Consider a $100 standing loan for which the principal is renewed automatically at the end of the year, and the interest rate is fully inflation-compensated. The real interest rate is 3 percent per annum and the expected and actual inflation rate is 20 percent. Applying relation (5.2), the nominal interest rate on the loan is

$$r = (1+0.03)(1+0.20) - 1 = 0.236 = 23.6\%$$

Thus, the interest expense at the end of the year is \$23.60. Applying relation (5.3),

$$rA = 0.20 \times 100 + 0.03 [(1+0.20)100]$$
$$= \$20.00 + \$3.60 = \$23.60$$

Thus, the interest expense comprises \$20 inflation-compensation on the principal and \$3.60 real interest payment. To put it differently, the \$100 outstanding principal should have appreciated by the end of the year to \$120, but it remains \$100, because \$20 has been repaid through nominal interest expense.

It should be noted that the higher the inflation rate, the larger the fraction of principal repayment embodied in the nominal interest rate. Suppose $p = 0.50$ in the former example, then interest expense is

$$rA = 0.50 \times 100 + 0.03[(1+0.50)100]$$
$$= \$50.00 + \$4.50 = \$54.50$$

The nominal interest rate includes a fraction of loan repayment irrespective of whether the rate is fixed for the whole loan term or the rate varies (floats). Varying interest agreements only shorten the period for which the nominal interest rate is set. Let us mention that in real life, the market rates of interest do not necessarily follow exactly the rates implied by relation (5.2) (for a recent review, see Sundell, 1983).

5.2 CASH FLOW FROM INVESTMENT FINANCED BY INSTALLMENT LOAN

A proposed investment is usually evaluated by its economic profitability. There is, however, another criterion to be considered—the impact of the proposed investment on the financial position of the firm. The financial position of a firm is hampered when, in a given period, cash flow from the investment is negative; that is, the receipts are lower than the summation of costs and payments on the loan financing the investment. During a period of inflation, this aspect becomes of special importance because of the specific behavior of nominal interest.

Table 5.1   Cash Flow from Investment and Installment Loan

Year (end)	0	1	2	3	4
Price index	100.00	120.00	144.00	172.80	207.36
Investment	$(1,000)	$ 338.40	$ 406.08	$ 487.30	$ 584.76
Loan[a]	1,000	(412.93)	(412.93)	(412.93)	(412.93)
Net cash flow	—	(74.53)	(6.05)	74.37	171.83

[a]Amortization factor based on 23.6 percent interest.

Consider first a period of stable prices. An investment of $1,000, with anticipated end-of-year net cash inflow of $282 for four years and a salvage value of zero, serves for illustration. Suppose the investment is financed by a four-year installment loan at 3 percent interest per annum. The annual end-of-year repayment of the loan, using an amortization table, is $269. Thus, the anticipated annual net cash inflow is $13 ($282−$269), ignoring uncertainty and income tax. The investment is economically sound and its impact on the firm's financial position is beneficial because there is an annual net cash inflow.

Consider now the same investment and loan under inflationary conditions, where the price level of all goods is anticipated to rise by 20 percent per annum in the next four years. Because of the anticipated inflation, the interest on the loan is set at the following rate:

$$(1+0.03)\ (1+0.20)\ -\ 1\ =\ 0.236\ =\ 23.6\%$$

The annual end-of-year payment of the installment loan at 23.6 percent interest, is $412.93. The pre-inflation end-of-year cash inflow of $282 will rise every year by 20 percent. The corresponding anticipated cash flow is presented in table 5.1. As can be seen, in the first two years the loan repayment is higher than the investment's cash inflow, and vice versa in the last two years.

The investment is still economically sound because nothing has changed—the investment's internal rate of return and the loan's cost did not change in real terms (for a proof, see Shashua and Goldschmidt, 1984). However, the cash deficit in the early years of the investment's life must be refinanced from outside sources, adversely affecting the liquidity position of the firm, as shown in the next section.

Table 5.2   Cash Flow from $1,000 Investment Financed by Installment Loan, Case of Zero Profit

Year (end)	0	1	2	3	4
Price Index	100.00	120.00	144.00	172.80	207.36
A. Cash flow					
Investment	$(1,000)	$322.84	$387.40	$464.88	$557.86
Loan[a]	1,000	(412.93)	(412.93)	(412.93)	(412.93)
Net cash flow	—	(90.09)	(25.53)	51.95	144.93
B. Needs for short-		(90.09)			
term loans[b]		× 1.236 =	(111.35)		
			(136.88)		
			× 1.236 =	(169.18)	
				(117.23)	
				× 1.236 =	(144.90)
					—
Cumulative needs		90.09	136.88	117.23	—

[a]Amortization factor based on 23.6 percent interest.
[b]The short-term loans bear 23.6 percent interest.

5.3 DETERMINING INFLATION-INDUCED NEEDS FOR SHORT-TERM LOANS

The cash deficit generated by the investment that is financed by a loan must be financed by short-term loans. Such loans usually cost more than long-term loans used for financing investments. The example in section 5.2 is used for determining the needs for short-term loans. To simplify the illustration, it is assumed that the annual profit from the investment is distributed as dividends (thus retained earnings are zero) and that the cost of the short-term loans is equal to the cost of the original loan—that is, the nominal interest rate on both loans is 23.6 percent per annum.

Consider a $1,000 investment that is financed by a $1,000 installment loan, the cash flow of which is presented in section A of table 5.2. The net present value of this investment is zero, using 23.6 percent discounting rate because the profit is not retained, compared to the investment presented in table 5.1, where the profit is retained. Calculation of the needs for short-term loans is illustrated in section B of table 5.2. The $90.09 cash deficit in the first year is financed by a short-term loan, bearing 23.6 percent interest. At the end of the second year, the need for short-term loans is composed of $90.09

from the previous year, plus the interest on it, which total $111.35, plus $25.53 current deficit. The needs in the third year decline because of the cash surplus, and in the fourth year the short-term loans are repaid.

The cumulative needs increase in the early years, decline later on, and reach zero level at the end of the investment's life because the profit level is zero. When profit is retained, as illustrated in table 5.1, the cumulative needs at the last year will end as a surplus. If the cost of the short-term loans is higher than the cost of the original loan, the cumulative needs will be larger than those illustrated in table 5.2, ending with a loss that must be covered from another source. (This subject is further discussed in section 6.3.)

5.4 INVESTMENT FINANCED BY VARYING-INTEREST AND INDEXED LOANS

In a period of inflation, lenders must adjust their interest rates to safeguard their capital against erosion. Two procedures are often used for such adjustment, varying (floating) interest rate and indexation.

Under a varying interest agreement the interest rate is reset at specified time intervals; that is, the interest rate on the loan is adjusted to the market situation at the beginning of each designated period. Under indexed loans, on the other hand, each pre-inflation payment on the loan is adjusted according to a specified price index (section 6.1), and there is no deviation between actual and expected inflation. The use of these types of loans in financing the previous illustrative investment is examined below.

Consider the previous example of investment under stable price conditions (section 5.2). The $1,000 four-year proposed investment is financed by a $1,000 installment loan bearing 3 percent interest per annum. The annual cash flow under constant price conditions is presented in section A of table 5.3. Two alternative procedures to safeguard the real value of the loan in case of inflation are analyzed. The loan agreement, under both procedures, is based on the loan repayment schedule which is prepared for stable price conditions, as presented in table 5.3, but the lender may add to the loan agreement a clause that enables him to vary the interest according to inflationary conditions that might exist in the future, or a clause that enables the lender to index each loan payment to the inflation rate.

Table 5.3 Cash Flow from $1,000 Investment Financed by Loans

Year (end)	1	2	3	4
A. Stable price conditions				
(1) Opening balance of loan	$1,000.00	$760.97	$514.77	$261.18
(2) Investment, net receipts	$282.00	$282.00	$282.00	$282.00
(3) Principal repayment	$(239.03)	$(246.20)	$(253.59)	$(261.18)
(4) Interest (3% on row 1)	(30.00)	(22.83)	(15.44)	(7.84)
(5) Total payments	(269.09)	(269.03)	(269.03)	(269.03)
Net cash flow	12.97	12.97	12.97	12.97
B. Inflation 20%, varying-interest loan				
Price index	120.000	144.000	172.800	207.360
Investment, net receipts[a]	$338.40	$406.08	$487.30	$584.76
Principal repayment (row 3)	$(239.03)	$(246.20)	$(253.59)	$(261.18)
Interest (23.6% on row 1)[b]	(236.00)	(179.59)	(121.49)	(61.64)
Total payments	(475.03)	(425.79)	(375.08)	(322.82)
Net cash flow	(136.63)	(19.71)	112.22	261.94
C. Inflation 20%, indexed loan				
Investment, net receipts[a]	$338.40	$406.08	$487.30	$584.76
Payments on loan (row 5, indexed)	$(322.84)	$(387.40)	$(464.88)	$(557.86)
Net cash flow	15.56	18.68	22.42	26.90

[a]Row 1 multiplied by the price index and divided by 100.
[b]Inflation-compensated rate: $(1 + 0.03)(1 + 0.20) - 1 = 0.236$.

Suppose that inflation at 20 percent per annum actually occurs in each of the four years. Accordingly, the investment's net receipts increase by 20 percent per annum and the varying interest rate is set at

$$(1+0.03)(1+0.20) - 1 = 0.236 = 23.6\%$$

This interest rate is applied to the loan balance at the beginning of each year. Annual payments for the indexed loan are computed by indexing the payments under stable price conditions. The resulting cash flows for the investment and the two alternative loan agreements are presented in sections A and B of table 5.3.

The net cash flow for the two alternative loans (table 5.3) should be compared with the net cash inflow for the case of the installment loan in table 5.1. The cash deficit under the varying interest loan, in the first two years, is larger than under the installment loan, despite the equal interest rate (23.6 percent) in both cases. Cash flow under the indexed loan, on the other hand, is positive in all the years, as it was under stable price conditions. The resulting net cash flow under the indexed loan is equal to the pre-inflation annual figure of $12.97, inflated by the annual price index.

The net cash inflow under the three alternative loan agreements is comparable because these are based on equal conditions (principal and real interest rate are fully inflation-compensated); only the procedure of including the inflation factor in the loan repayments differs. Thus, checking the net cash inflow shows the advantage of the indexed loan for the borrower. Its superiority lies in the impact on the firm's financial position, given that inflation is anticipated correctly in setting the interest rates for the installment and varying-interest loans.

The indexed loan has an additional advantage—there is no need to predict the inflation rate while setting the interest rate, and the uncertainty which accompanies conventional loans in time of inflation is thus eliminated. This type of uncertainty is reduced under varying interest agreements because the term of resetting the interest rate is shorter—for example, each quarter in the varying scheme versus the whole term under a conventional loan. Whether the interest rate is fixed for the entire loan term or varying, inflation must somehow be predicted. Divergence of the actual inflation rate from the anticipated rate tends to produce windfall returns either for the borrower or for the lender.

5.5 INFLATION-INDUCED EFFECT OF DEBT ON THE LIQUIDITY POSITION

Financial liquidity is an important aspect in evaluating the economic and financial situation of a firm. This is evidenced by the widespread use of both the current ratio (current assets related to current liabilities) and the quick ratio (current assets less inventory related to current liabilities) in business and financial analysis. For example, the average current ratio for 2,400 companies in all United States industries in 1975 was about two, with a distribution between one and four (Foster, 1978, p. 179). A current ratio higher than one indicates that a portion of the current assets is financed by long-term funds, meaning that fixed assets are financed fully by long-term funds (equity and long-term loans).

The discussion in the preceding sections shows that inflation affects the cash flow from an investment that is financed by conventional loans (installment or varying interest). A cash deficit, which is created in early periods of the investment's life, is usually financed by short-term loans. Thus, the original long-term loan is partially substituted by short-term loans; the higher the inflation rate, the more accelerated this substitution becomes, weakening the liquidity position of the firm. To complete the analysis, the reflection of this phenomenon in the financial statements is illustrated below.

Suppose the proposed investment, which is presented in table 5.3, has been executed and that the anticipated events actually occurred. The ex-post results, at the end of the first year, will be recorded in the financial statements of the firm. To simplify, only those records which reflect the result of the execution of the investment are presented. To view the whole picture, these records must be added to the firm's financial statement which reflects the firm's activities without the investment. Corresponding financial statements for the case of stable price conditions, and for inflationary conditions—for the two types of loan agreements (varying interest and indexed)—are presented in table 5.4, assuming that the straight-line depreciation is used.

Consider first the financial statements under stable price level conditions, as shown in section A of table 5.4. The EBIDT—earnings before interest, depreciation, and tax (corresponding to the net receipts from the investment) is higher than (1) expenses, leaving $2 net income, and (2) cash outlays, leaving $12.97 surplus. Thus, the investment improved the firm's liquidity position. This is seen by the fact that the current assets (cash) are financed by a long-term

Table 5.4 Historical-Cost Financial Statements, a Year after Investment, Investment of $1,000

A. Stable price conditions

Income statement		Cash statement		Balance sheet, end of year			
EBIDT	282.00	EBIDT	282.00	Assets	1,000.00	Loan	1,000.00
Interest, 3%	(30.00)	Interest	(30.00)	Depreciation	(250.00)	Loan repayment	(239.03)
Depreciation	(250.00)	Loan repayment	(239.03)		750.00		760.97
Net income	2.00	Surplus	12.97	Cash	12.97	Retained income	2.00
					762.97		762.97

B. Inflation 20%, varying interest loan

Income statement		Cash statement		Balance sheet, end of year			
EBIDT	338.40	EBIDT	338.40	Assets	1,000.00	Loan	1,000.00
Interest, 23.6%	(236.00)	Interest	(236.00)	Depreciation	(250.00)	Loan repayment	(239.03)
Depreciation	(250.00)	Loan repayment	(239.03)		750.00		760.97
Net income (Loss)	(147.60)	Deficit	(136.63)	Loss	147.60	Short-term loan	136.63
		Short-term loan	136.63		897.60		897.60

C. Inflation 20%, indexed loan

Income statement		Cash statement		Balance sheet, end of year			
EBIDT	338.40	EBIDT	338.40	Assets	1,000.00	Loan	1,000.00
Interest, 3%	(36.00)	Interest	(36.00)	Depreciation	(250.00)	Indexation	200.00
Loan indexation	(200.00)	Loan repayment	(286.84)		750.00	Loan repayment	(286.84)
Depreciation	(250.00)	Surplus	15.56	Cash	15.56		913.16
Net income (Loss)	(147.60)			Loss	147.60		
					913.16		

EBIDT = earnings before interest, depreciation, and tax.
Source: Table 5.3.

loan. But interestingly enough, the same investment, financed by varying interest loan, worsened the firm's liquidity position under inflationary conditions as shown in section B of table 5.4. The fixed asset is financed by a $136.63 short-term loan, despite the fact that it was originally financed by a long-term loan. Even when the asset is revalued (from recorded value of $750 to $900 current value), it is partially financed by a short-term loan. Under the indexed loan (section C of table 5.4), on the other hand, the investment improved the firm's liquidity position.

SIX

LIQUIDITY ASPECTS OF LOANS
DURING INFLATION

The preceding chapter illustrates the damaging effect of inflation on financial liquidity of a leveraged firm. It has also been shown that no damage results when investments are financed by indexed loans. This is because loan indexation causes the repayment schedule during inflation to be similar in nature to the investment's cash flow.

Loan indexation is commonly practiced in countries where inflation is persistent and high, but it is not practiced in the United States. The fact that even relatively low inflation in the United States brought about liquidity burdens to firms, especially to farms (as shown in chapter 8), suggests the usefulness of adopting the practice of loan indexation for investments. The first three sections of this chapter are devoted to a description of indexed loans and their liquidity aspects.

Financing investments by conventional loans in comparison to indexed loans ultimately calls for additional funds (usually short-term loans). Since these funds impose a financial burden on the firm, a measure for evaluating the relative magnitude of these needs is devised. This measure can be used as a supplement to the conventional measure of economic cost, in evaluating alternative loans.

6.1 DESCRIPTION OF INDEX-LINKED LOANS

To safeguard the lender and the borrower against the effect of inflation on the repayment of loans, a "linkage" clause can be inserted into the loan agreement. Linking both principal and interest to a price level index is commonly practiced in countries such as Brazil and

Israel (where inflation is persistent and high), and it has been legally allowed in the United States since 1977 (White, 1981). Under index-linked loans the contracted payments, principal, and interest are linked to changes in price level. The contracted payments are based on inflation-free interest and are indexed in each payment period to safeguard the principal against inflation and to keep the real interest intact. From the accounting point of view, the balance of the outstanding loan is indexed as well (Aharoni and Ophir, 1967).

For simplifying the calculations, index-linked loans are usually paid by equal principal payments rather than by equal payments of principal plus interest, as with conventional installment loans. The indexation procedure must determine the values to be indexed (principal, interest, or a portion of these), the price index to be used (consumer price index, or other specific index), and the binding dates of payments and index announcement.

Index-linked loans have several advantages. First, there is a clear distinction between real interest expenses and loan repayment. Second, the repayment schedule of the loan conforms with the returns of the assets which are financed by the loan, assuming that there is a correlation between the corresponding price levels. This aspect has an important effect on the firm's financial position. Third, the real inflation-free interest rate is stated explicitly, avoiding the need to base the nominal interest rate on expectations regarding the inflation rate. This aspect reduces the uncertainty in respect to the real cost of a loan. In turn, it eliminates the occurrence of windfall returns, either to borrower or to lender, which result from the divergence of the actual inflation rate from the anticipated rate.

To illustrate the indexation procedure, consider a $100 loan to be repaid, under stable price conditions, by two end-of-year equal payments of $50. The inflation-free interest is 5 percent, to be paid at the end of each year, on the outstanding loan balance. Both principal and interest are index-linked. The corresponding repayment schedules are presented in table 6.1. The indexed payments are determined by multiplying the contracted payments by the corresponding price index. The indexation can also be viewed as follows: at the end of the first year the $100 original principal is indexed to become $120, of which $60 is repaid. The $120 principal earned 5 percent real interest which means a $6 interest payment. The $60 outstanding balance, at the beginning of the second year, is treated in the same manner at the end of the second year.

Table 6.1 Actual Repayment of an Indexed Loan, $100 Repaid over Two Years

Year (end)	0	1	2
Price index	100	120	144
A. Contracted payments (planned for stable price level)			
Principal repayment		$50.00	$50.00
Interest, 5%		5.00	2.50
Total payment		55.00	52.50
B. Indexed payments (actual inflation-compensated)[a]			
Principal repayment		$60.00	$72.00
Interest		6.00	3.60
Total payment		66.00	75.60
Outstanding balance			
Original	$100	$50	$ —
Indexed	100	60	—

[a]The contracted amounts multiplied by the price index and divided by 100.

6.2 DEBT SERVICE OF INDEXED VERSUS CONVENTIONAL LOANS

The service of a conventional loan is determined by the contracted nominal interest rate which embodies real interest plus a premium for the expected inflation. The actual ex-post cost is equal to the ex-ante contracted cost. The same holds for a varying interest agreement, but only for the period for which the interest payment is specified. The cost of an indexed loan, on the other hand, is determined by the contracted real interest rate and the actual inflation rate. Therefore, the actual cost of the loan depends on the ex-post inflation rate.

Under an indexed loan, the borrower's obligation increases through the indexation of the loan's outstanding balance. Because of the accrual principle, this increased obligation is considered as an expense by conventional accounting practices. Thus, the total recorded expenses of an indexed loan, in a given period, is the summation of the indexed interest payment and the indexation differentials of the principal.

Consider the previous example of a $100 loan to be repaid in two end-of-year equal payments at 5 percent real interest rate. Suppose that both the expected and the actual inflation rates coincide at 20 percent per annum. This loan is used for illustrating the annual

Table 6.2 Repayment and Expenses of a Loan under Two Contracts, $100 Repaid over Two Years

Year (end)	0	1	2
Price index	100	120	144
A. Indexed contract (table 6.1)			
Total payments		$66.00	$75.60
Recorded expenses:			
Interest		6.00	3.60
Indexation differential[a]		20.00	12.00
Total expenses		26.00	15.60
B. Conventional contract			
Outstanding balance	$100.00	$50.00	$ —
Payments:			
Principal repayment		$50.00	$50.00
Interest, 26%		26.00	13.00
Total payments		76.00	63.00
Interest on short-term loan[b]		—	2.60
Recorded expenses:			
Interest		26.00	15.60

[a]In year 1: $10 on repaid principal and $10 on outstanding principal; in year 2: $12 on repaid principal.
[b]The $10 difference between the $76 total payments on the conventional loan and the $66 on the indexed loan is financed by short-term loan to enable comparison.

expenses under two alternative repayment contracts: (1) an indexed contract at 5 percent interest where both principal and interest are indexed (table 6.1), and (2) a conventional contract at 26 percent interest (5 percent, inflation-compensated) on the loan balance at the beginning of the year. The corresponding figures are presented in table 6.2.

The total payment under the conventional contract, at the end of the first year, is $76, whereas under the indexed contract it is $66. In order to compare the two contracts, and assuming that the loan finances a given investment, the difference between the payments must be financed from an outside source by a short-term loan. To make the comparison between the two contracts meaningful, it is assumed that the interest on the short-term loan is equal to that on the original loan; that is, 26 percent per annum on $10, which is $2.60. Thus, the total interest expense on the conventional contract is $15.60, which equals the recorded expenses under the indexed contract. But there is an important difference between the two contracts—the conventional loan implies a need for supplementary short-term financing. This subject is further analyzed in the next section.

6.3 LIQUIDITY ASPECTS OF LOANS: INDEXED VERSUS CONVENTIONAL

The preceding discussion shows that the repayment schedule of an indexed loan differs from that of a comparable conventional loan. This difference has an important implication for financial management.

Consider the two types of loans, which are equal in all aspects under stable price level conditions; under inflationary conditions, however, these loans differ substantially. Taking out a conventional loan instead of an indexed loan means that additional funds must be obtained in the early years of the loan term—funds which must be repaid in later years. In order to weigh the advantages of an indexed loan as against a conventional loan, two alternative financial schemes must be compared, an indexed loan and a conventional loan plus supplementary short-term loans. Let us compare these two schemes by first calculating the need for short-term loans.

Consider a $1,000 loan to be repaid in four end-of-period equal payments. The inflation-free interest rate is 1 percent per period, calculated on the opening balance and paid at the end of each period. The corresponding repayment schedules, under conditions of both stable prices and inflation, are presented in table 6.3, assuming a 10 percent price level rise per period and interest rate of 11.1 percent (1 percent inflation-compensated) per period.

The cash shortage resulting from the difference between the two repayment schedules is assumed to be financed by short-term loans at 11.1 percent interest per period, similar to the illustration in table 5.2. As the cash shortage prevails for two periods, the cumulative needs, including the period's cash shortage plus the outstanding short-term loans, "grows" in the second period from $75.00 to $105.02. In the next two periods the level of the cumulative needs declines because of the periodic cash surplus which allows partial repayment of the outstanding short-term loans. At the end of the loan term, the needs are nullified.

The figures in the bottom of table 6.3 show that when the loan is taken out under conventional agreement rather than as an indexed loan, management has to raise additional funds in the first three periods (475.00, $105.02, and $82.77, respectively). The cumulative needs reach the level of zero at the end of the loan's term, because the real cost of the two finance schemes is the same (1 percent real

Table 6.3 Calculating the Needs for Short-Term Loans, Repayment of a $1,000 Loan under Conventional and Indexed Contract

Period (end)	0	1	2	3	4
A. Stable price conditions					
Principal repayment		$250.00	$250.00	$250.00	$250.00
Interest, 1%		10.00	7.50	5.00	2.50
Total		260.00	257.00	255.00	252.50
B. Inflationary conditions (10% per annum)					
Price index	100.000	110.000	121.000	133.100	146.410
Conventional loan:					
Principal repayment		$250.00	$250.00	$250.00	$250.00
Interest, 11.1%		111.00	83.25	55.50	27.75
Total		361.00	333.25	305.50	277.75
Indexed loan[a]		286.00	311.56	339.41	369.69
Cash shortage		75.00	21.69	(33.91)	(91.94)
Needs for short-term loans[b]		75.00 × 1.111 =	83.33	116.67	91.94
			21.69	(33.91)	(91.94)
			105.02 × 1.111 =	82.77 × 1.111 =	—
Cumulative needs (outstanding short-term loans)					
In nominal dollars		$75.00	$105.02	$82.77	—
In constant prices of period 0[c]		68.18	86.79	62.19	
Relative to the $1,000 loan		6.12%	8.68%	6.22%	

[a]Total under stable price conditions multiplied by the price index and divided by 100.
[b]The short-term loans bear 11.1 percent interest per period.
[c]Nominal values divided by the price index and multiplied by 100.

interest per period), indicating that the economic cost of both schemes is identical. As can be seen, the cumulative needs rise in early years of the loan term and subside later on. To speak in graphic terms, in general, the cumulative needs assume the shape of a bell.

6.4 A MEASURE FOR EVALUATING THE LIQUIDITY BURDEN OF A LOAN

As the repayment schedule of an indexed loan is assumed to move concurrently with the expected cash flow generated by the investment, the repayment schedule of other loans can be compared with that of an indexed loan. This reasoning provides the basis for developing a simple measure for evaluating the relative amount of short-term interim funds needed by a proposed loan, under a given anticipated inflation rate. In other words, this measure is designed for evaluating the liquidity aspects of a proposed loan, where the liquidity is relative to an indexed loan or to an investment to be financed by loans.

The proposed measure is defined as:

$$\text{LBA} = \frac{1}{nA} \sum \frac{\Delta R_t}{(1 + p)^t} \tag{6.1}$$

where LBA = liquidity burden, average for the loan's period, in constant prices of period 0, on \$1 loan,

ΔR_t = difference between the cumulative service of the loan under analysis (including the interest expenses at the market rate) in period t, to that of an indexed loan,

A = amount of the loan at $t = 0$,

n = number of loan repayment periods.

The liquidity burden in period t, in constant prices of period 0, on a \$1 loan, is

$$\text{LB}_t = \frac{1}{A} \cdot \frac{\Delta R_t}{(1 + p)^t} \tag{6.2}$$

The measure of LBA indicates the additional uncertainty due to the investment under conditions of inflation and the prevailing mode of debt finance. When the additional uncertainty cannot be quantified, the proposed measure can be used, in an inflationary period, as a supplementary indicator in evaluating proposed investments financed by loans.

Consider the example in table 6.3, where the cumulative needs for short-term loans ΔR_t, are presented in nominal dollars at the foot of the table. Relation (6.2) is used to enable a comparison of these needs with the amount of the $1,000 original loan as follows: first the figures are transformed into constant prices stated in period 0 dollars, as presented near the bottom of table 6.3; second, each figure is divided by 1,000, to arrive at relative figures as presented in the last row in table 6.3. Applying relation (6.1), the measure of the average liquidity burden for the loan's period is

$$(68.18 + 86.79 + 62.19 + 0)/(1,000 \times 4) = 0.05429 = 5.43\%$$

The liquidity burden per period is, on the average, 5.43 percent on the original long-term loan. In other words, if the $1,000 investment is financed by a conventional loan, the firm must raise, on the average, short-term loans in the amount of $54.30 each period, assuming that the pattern of the cash flow from the investment is equal to that of an indexed loan.

6.5 FACTORS AFFECTING THE INFLATION-INDUCED LIQUIDITY BURDEN OF LOANS

The measures proposed in relations (6.1) and (6.2) are used in this section for evaluating the effects of some factors on the liquidity burden of loans—that is, on the relative needs for short-term loans arising from a non-indexed loan compared to the indexed loan. The example in table 6.3 is used as a bench mark for illustrating the effect of the following factors on the liquidity burden of a conventional loan: (1) the rate of inflation, which is set at 30 percent per period instead of 10 percent; (2) the lifespan of the loan, which is set at 10 periods for both loans instead of four periods; (3) the real cost of the short-term loans—the nominal interest is set at 20 percent per period instead of 11.1 percent; and (4) the real cost of the conventional loan—the nominal rate is set at 10 percent per period (that is, a real rate of zero) instead of 11.1 percent, whereas the real interest rate on both the indexed loan and the short-term loans is left at 1 percent per period.

Consider first the effect of an increase in the inflation rate on the liquidity burden of the loan that is illustrated in table 6.3. Increasing the inflation rate from 10 percent to 30 percent per period raises the average liquidity burden from 5.43 percent to 12.84 percent. The periodic liquidity burden of the two cases (30 percent versus 10 percent)—that is, the cumulative need for short-term loans—is depicted

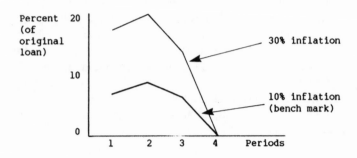

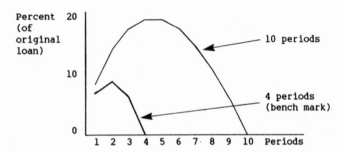

Fig. 6.1 Liquidity burden of a conventional loan:
a case of equal economic costs (bench mark in table 6.3)

in the upper graph in figure 6.1 (the corresponding figures are presented in table 6.4). As can be seen, in both cases the curve for the periodic liquidity burden is bellshaped; the 30 percent inflation curve, throughout, is above the 10 percent curve. Increasing the lifespan of the loan has a similar effect, as can be seen in the lower graph in figure 6.1, where the 10-period loan is compared with the bench mark illustration of the four-period loan.

In the above two illustrations, the real interest rate on the short-term loans was set to be the same as that on the original loans. Therefore, the economic cost of the conventional loan is equal to that of the indexed loan. An increase in either inflation rate or lifespan of the loan affects the liquidity burden of the conventional loan—the higher the inflation rate and the longer the life of the loan, the higher the burden. The burden declines to zero at the end of the loans' period.

The effect of a change in the interest rates on both the liquidity burden and the economic cost of a conventional loan relative to an indexed agreement is shown in the next two illustrations.

Table 6.4 Liquidity Burden of a Conventional Loan under Four Cases, Percentages Related to the Original Long-Term Loan

			Factor Analyzed			
	Bench Mark (table 6.3)	Inflation Rate	Term of Loans[a]	Interest on Short Loans	Interest on the Conventional Loan
A. Conditions under analysis					
Inflation rate	10%	30%	10%	10%	10%
Loans' period	4 periods	4 periods	10 periods	4 periods	4 periods
Interest on short-term loans	11.1%	11.1%	11.1%	20.0%	11.1%
Interest on conventional loan	11.1	11.1	11.1	11.1	10.0
B. Results					
Period 1	6.82%	17.31%	8.18%	6.82%	5.91%
Period 2	8.68	20.41	13.88	9.23	7.08
Period 3	6.19	13.63	17.41	7.52	4.19
Last period[b]	—	—	—	1.93	(2.56)
Average	5.43	12.84	12.56	6.37	3.65

[a]The corresponding percentages for periods 4 to 10 are: 19.02, 18.95, 17.42, 14.50, 10.57, 5.66, 0.
[b]Period 4 except for the third column.

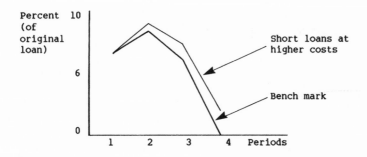

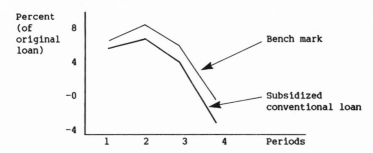

Fig. 6.2 Liquidity burden of a conventional loan:
a case of nonequal economic costs (bench mark in table 6.3)

Consider first a case where the marginal interest on the short-term loans, including the costs involved in receiving such credit, is set at 20 percent per period (instead of 11.1 percent as assumed in the previous analyses), but the real interest rate on the original loan is not changed. This change in the cost of short-term loans raises both the liquidity burden and the economic cost of the conventional loan relative to the indexed loan, as shown in the upper graph in figure 6.2. The liquidity burden is higher and the need for short-term loans is not nullified at the end of the loan's period. Since the interest on the short-term loans is higher than the interest on the original loan, the difference of 1.93 percent (table 6.4) indicates the difference in the economic cost of the two loans, stated at the end of the loan's period, in price level of period 0.

A case of a subsidized conventional loan is illustrated in the lower graph in figure 6.2. In this case the conventional loan bears zero real interest rate (10 percent inflation-compensated rate), whereas the bench mark indexed loan and the interim short-term loans bear 1 percent real interest rate. The conventional loan causes a liquidity burden of only 3.65 percent per period (foot of table 6.4) and its economic cost is lower than the indexed loan by $25.60 (2.56 percent). In other words, the borrower has two measures for evaluating this loan: the loan is cheaper by 2.56 percent, but it requires interim finance of short-term loans at the average volume of 3.65 percent, compared to the indexed loan.

Finally, let us mention that including income tax in the calculations will not affect the results illustrated above as long as the real interest rate under both financing schemes is the same. This is because the sum of the interest payments and the accrued indexed differentials on the principal of the indexed loan is equal to the total interest payments on the original conventional loan and the interim loans (table 6.2). In both cases these are tax-deductible expenses. However, when the real interest rates on the loans differ, then after-tax expenses should be considered in the case of a taxpaying firm.

To sum up, the analysis in this section shows that the higher the inflation rate and the rate of interest on short-term loans, and the longer the lifespan of the conventional original loan, the larger the needs for interim short-term loans, and hence, the greater the deterioration of the firm's liquidity.

EFFECT OF INFLATION ON INCOME TAX LIABILITY

The analysis in the preceding chapters ignored the marginal effect of income tax under inflation. The purpose of this chapter is to evaluate the effect of the existing income tax rules during times of inflation on the profitability of investment and its effect on financing policy of the firm.

It is well known that equity is eroded by tax during inflation. On the other hand, the analysis in this chapter indicates that debt finance enjoys a net tax benefit. This net benefit induces firms to increase their financial leverage, which in turn raises the liquidity burden (the ratio of short-term to long-term loans).

Based on the analysis in this chapter, the break-even financial leverage for zero tax benefit under inflation is provided to help management in their financing policy and to enable policymakers to understand the effect of tax and inflation on investments.

7.1 ILLUSTRATING THE INFLATION TAX EFFECT

A simple example, where the results are self-evident, is presented to illustrate the effect of inflation on tax liabilities that result from the prevailing income tax regulations. To simplify the presentation, the asset is financed totally by a loan and both the return on the asset and the interest rate on the loan, in real terms, equal zero. Further, the inflation is fully anticipated and is assumed to be neutral—that is, all the prices increase by the same rate.

Consider a two-year $1,000 asset financed by a $1,000 loan. The pre-inflation return on the asset is equal to the interest on the loan. As the real return is zero, the annual gross return of $500 is equal to the depreciation used to reduce the loan. Under inflation of 20 percent per annum, the gross returns (earnings before interest, depreciation, and tax—EBIDT) will grow from \$500 to \$600 in the first year, and to \$720 in the second year. These figures, which are equal to the current cost of depreciation, are used to repay the loan. The corresponding financial statements for the two years, assuming straight-line depreciation, are presented in table 7.1.

Real income in the example is equal to zero; hence, the correct income tax liability should also be equal to zero. Table 7.1 shows that the present value of the historical-cost net income, before tax, is −\$13.89, using the 20 percent nominal rate of return for discounting. This figure indicates an extra tax liability (because the correct tax is zero), resulting from the understatement of the correct tax liability. In this example, the firm will have a tax benefit, in present value terms, of −\$13.89m, where m is the relevant rate of income tax, given that the firm has tax liabilities resulting from its other activities.

Measuring the Net Change in Tax Liability

According to the existing income tax regulations, income is taxed after allowance for historical depreciation and interest expense actually paid. The correct net income, however, is arrived at after deducting current depreciation and imputed real interest. In other words, the actual tax liability is determined by

$$D_h + I_a$$

whereas the correct tax liability is determined by

$$D_c + I_r$$

where D_h, D_c = depreciation charges, historical and current, respectively,

I_a, I_r = interest expenses, actual and real, respectively.

The net change in tax liability is therefore

$$(D_h + I_a) - (D_c + I_r) \tag{7.1}$$

or

$$(D_h - D_c) - (I_r - I_a) \tag{7.2}$$

where $(D_h - D_c)$ = difference in tax liability due to depreciation,

$(I_r - I_a)$ = difference in tax liability due to interest.

It is interesting to note that the level of the first term in relation (7.2) is affected by the assets' lifespan, whereas the second term is

Table 7.1   Financial Statements and Income Tax Liability under Inflation, Investment of $1,000

Year (end)	0	1	2
Price index	100.000	120.000	144.000
Cash statements			
EBIDT		$600	$720
Interest, 20%		(200)	(120)
Surplus		400	600
Loan repayment		(400)	(600)
Retained cash		—	—
Balance sheets			
Assets, historical	$1,000	$500	$ —
Assets, current	1,000	600	—
Loan	1,000	600	—
Income statements, historical-cost			
EBIDT		$600	$720
Interest		(200)	(120)
Depreciation		(500)	(500)
Net income before tax		(100)	100
Present value, 20%	$(13.89)		
Income tax liabilities: actual vs. correct			
(1) Depreciation, current		$600	$720
Depreciation, historical		(500)	(500)
Difference		100	220
Present value, 20%	$236.11		
(2) Interest, real, 0%		$ —	$ —
Interest, actual, 20%		(200)	(120)
Difference		(200)	(120)
Present value	(250.00)		
(3) Net tax liability, (1)–(2)		(100)	100
Present value, 20%	(13.89)		

EBIDT = earnings before interest, depreciation, and tax.

not. The meaning of each of the two terms is discussed in the next two sections.

Relation (7.2) is applied to the numerical example at the foot of table 7.1. As can be seen, the net change in tax liability is −$13.98 in present value terms.

The source of the net change in tax liability can be seen by inspecting the balance sheets in table 7.1. The loan balance at the end of the first year is equal to the current value of the asset. This situation is true in all cases where the net income in real terms is distributed as dividends and is not retained within the firm. This situation results from the fact that the loan finances the full value of the asset even though this value is not recorded in the historical-cost balance sheet. In other words, the interest on the loan that finances the nonrecorded appreciation of the asset is tax deductible, whereas the corresponding appreciation in the asset's value is not recorded as taxable income. The interest on the loan that finances the nonrecorded asset value provides the extra or the net change in tax liability.

7.2 EQUITY EROSION DUE TO OVERTAXATION

During a period of inflation, equity is eroded because of overtaxation of income that is generated by assets financed by equity. The level of equity erosion depends on the type of asset in which the equity is invested and on the rate of inflation. The shorter the lifespan of the asset and the higher the inflation rate, the higher the overtaxation and the resulting equity erosion. The analysis below is applied to fixed assets, but the results shed light on the situation regarding financial assets and inventories.

According to Shashua and Goldschmidt (1983, p. 380), the erosion in a given year, on the acquisition value of a depreciable asset, is

$$E_n = md_n[(1 + p)^n - 1]A \qquad (7.3)$$

where E_n = erosion at end of year n,
$\quad$ m = rate of income tax,
$\quad$ d_n = depreciation rate on historical acquisition cost, for year n,
$(1 + p)^n$ = compounding the depreciation by p for n periods,
$\quad$ A = acquisition value of asset = invested equity.

Using the data in table 7.1, and given that the income tax rate is 50 percent, the erosion in the two years is as follows:

$$E_1 = 0.50 \times 0.50 \ [(1 + 0.20) - 1]1000 = \$50$$
$$E_2 = 0.50 \times 0.50 \ [(1 + 0.20)^2 - 1]1000 = \$110$$

Consider first a one-year fixed asset; that is, an asset with a lifespan of no more than one year. Thus, the depreciation rate is one and relation (7.3) will take the form of

$$E = mpA \qquad (7.4)$$

The erosion of equity is equal to the inflation-compensation on the acquisition value multiplied by the tax rate. For example, $1,000 equity is invested in a one-year asset. Under an inflation rate of 20 percent and a 50 percent income tax rate, the erosion is

$$E = 0.50 \times 0.20 \times 1,000 = \$100$$

Relation (7.4) also suits the case of inventories which are accounted for by the first-in-first-out (FIFO) method, where the cost of materials used stands for the depreciation rate of one, and the inflation rate is for the turnover period of inventories. Furthermore, relation (7.4) suits the case of a one-year financial asset redeemed or renewed within one year.

To further clarify the measurement of equity erosion on one-year assets, the corresponding financial statement for the two types of investments are presented in table 7.2, for the cases of inflation and stable prices. The gross receipts in the examples are designed to cover the real depreciation and a real return on capital of 5 percent, in the case of the fixed asset, and to cover the inflation-compensated returns on capital of 5 percent, in the case of the financial asset. In both cases, the equity erosion is equal to $100.

Consider now a nondepreciable asset, such as land or an investment in a subsidiary. Since there is no depreciation (the depreciation rate is zero), relation (7.3) will show that the corresponding periodic erosion is also zero; equity erosion may occur only upon the sale of the asset, when tax on capital gains is paid (see table 7.2, nondepreciable asset case).

The General Case

The present value of capital erosion under the continuous case, under the assumption of exponential depreciation, is

$$PV(E) = m \int_0^\infty \frac{be^{-bt}}{e^{ht}} \, dt - m \int_0^\infty \frac{be^{-bt} e^{pt}}{e^{ht}} \, dt$$

$$= m[\frac{b}{h + b} - \frac{b}{h + b - p}] \qquad (7.5)$$

The first term in the bracket represents the present value of the nominal (historical) depreciation schedule and the second term the present value of the current depreciation schedule, using the dis-

Table 7.2 Financial Statements for a Going Concern, Three Types of Assets Financed by Equity, Each $1,000

	One Year Fixed Asset		One Year Financial Asset		Nondepreciable Asset	
	No Inflation	Inflation 20%	No Inflation	Inflation 20%	No Inflation	Inflation 20%[a]
Historical-cost income statements						
EBIDT	$1,050	$1,260	$ 50	$ 260	$ 50	$ 60
Depreciation	(1,000)	(1,000)	—	—	—	—
Net income, before tax	50	260	50	260	50	60
Income tax, 50%	(25)	(130)	(25)	(130)	(25)	(30)
Net income, after tax	25	130	25	130	25	30
Dividends	(25)	(30)	(25)	(30)	(25)	(30)
Retained earnings	—	100	—	100	—	—
Cash statements						
Retained earnings	$ —	$ 100	$ —	$ 100	$ —	$ —
Depreciation	1,000	1,000	—	—	—	—
Redeemed principal	—	—	1,000	1,000	—	—
Total funds	1,000	1,100	1,000	1,100	—	—
Renewal	1,000	1,200	1,000	1,200	—	—
Balance = erosion	—	(100)	—	(100)	—	—

[a]At the end of the first year the land value is $1,200. If it is sold, $200 capital gains are taxable.
EBIDT = earnings before interest, depreciation and tax.

counting rate h, where PV(E) = present value of equity erosion due to depreciation,

> m = rate of income tax,
> b = depreciation rate of the exponential type such as declining balance,[1]
> h = nominal cost of capital.

It should be noted that

$$\frac{b}{h + b} = PV(D)_h \qquad (7.6)$$

$$\frac{b}{h + b - p} = PV(D)_{h-p} \qquad (7.7)$$

PV(D)$_h$ = present value of nominal depreciation schedule, using the discounting rate h.

Relation (7.2) is devised for the continuous case, but the result, as stated by relations (7.6) and (7.7), is applicable to the discrete case and for a finite lifespan.[2]

7.3 TAX REBATE ON LOANS

During a period of inflation the interest on loans embodies a premium for the decline in the purchasing power of the loan. This premium or inflation-compensation is not a cost but rather a loan repayment (section 5.1); therefore, the difference between the actual and the correct tax liabilities due to interest is $I_r - I_a$ as stated in section 7.1. The calculation of this difference is illustrated in table 7.1 for the case of an individual asset and zero real interest rate. The calculations show that the tax liability due to interest is larger than that due to depreciation.

The General Case

Parallel to the computation of the present value of equity erosion in the preceding section, the present value of the tax rebate on loans, under the continuous case, is

$$PV(B) = m\int_0^\infty \frac{he^{-bt}e^{pt}}{e^{ht}} \, dt - m\int_0^\infty \frac{(h-p)e^{-bt}e^{pt}}{e^{ht}} \quad (7.8)$$

$$= m\int_0^\infty \frac{pe^{-bt}e^{pt}}{e^{ht}} = \frac{mp}{h+b-p}$$

The first term represents the present value of the tax rebate on the actual interest payments on the loan that finances the asset, and the second term represents the present value of the tax rebate required on the real interest charges, where PV(B) = present value of tax rebate due to interest.

Net Benefit

The difference between the tax rebate due to interest (relation 7.8) and the equity erosion due to depreciation (relation 7.5) is the net benefit from the inflation tax effect. The present value of this benefit is

$$PV \text{ (Net benefit)} = \frac{mp}{h+b-p} + \frac{mb}{h+b} - \frac{mb}{h+b-p} \quad (7.9)$$

$$= \frac{mph}{(h+b-p)(h+b)}$$

The annual net benefit, indexed to inflation, is derived by multiplying relation (7.9) by the real rate, which is $h - p$. Assuming that the nominal interest rate is fully inflation-compensated, then

$$h - p = r^*,$$

and the annual net benefit is

$$\text{Annual net benefit} = \frac{mphr^*}{(r^* + b)(h + b)} \quad (7.10)$$

Relation (7.10) is always positive. This means that during inflation the tax rebate on interest is always higher than capital erosion, when fixed assets are financed totally by loans. In other words, under existing tax rules the marginal tax benefit from the loan is always higher than the erosion of equity.

Relation (7.10) indicates that the higher the rates of inflation and income tax and the longer the asset's lifespan (thus, the lower the depreciation rate) the higher the net benefit from tax. Furthermore, when the depreciation rate is zero, the annual net benefit is mp; when the rate is very high (a very short asset lifespan), the annual net benefit approaches zero.

7.4 THE BREAK-EVEN FINANCIAL LEVERAGE UNDER INFLATION

The discussion in the preceding section shows that firms have a net inflation tax benefit when depreciable assets are fully financed by loans. For the tax liability to be neutral to inflation, the net benefit should be zero. The equity erosion factor is related to the depreciation schedule of the asset and is not affected by whether the asset is financed by equity or by debt. The tax rebate on the loan, on the other hand, is related directly to the level of the loan.

For the net benefit to be zero, the tax rebate on loans should be equal to the equity erosion. Thus, the level of the tax liability due to interest should be set at a level equal to the level of tax liability due to depreciation. Using relation (7.2) the break-even level of liabilities is

$$f(I_a - I_r) = (D_c - D_h) \tag{7.11}$$

$$\text{and } f = \frac{(D_c - D_h)}{(I_a - I_r)} \tag{7.12}$$

where f = ratio of debt to assets = financial leverage required for zero net tax benefit.

The General Case

Under the continuous case, for the net benefit to be zero,

$$f \times PV(B) = - PV(E) \tag{7.13}$$

Note that the equity erosion is defined as a loss, whereas the tax rebate on the loan is defined as a gain. Inserting relations (7.5) and (7.8), into relation (7.13),

$$\frac{fmp}{h + a - p} = \frac{ma}{h + a - p} - \frac{ma}{h + a}$$

which yields

$$f = \frac{b}{h + b} = PV(D)_h \qquad (7.14)$$

For example, suppose $b = 0.30$, which means that about 78 percent of the original cost is depreciated in 5 years; and suppose $p = 20$ percent, and $h = 26$ percent corresponding to 5 percent real interest. The required financial leverage for zero net tax benefit is

$$f = \frac{0.30}{0.26 + 0.30} = 0.536$$

that is, 53.6 percent of the investment in depreciable assets should be financed by a loan.

Relation (7.14) implies the following conclusions: (1) The higher the inflation rate, the higher the tax benefit from the loan and hence the lower the break-even leverage; (2) the longer the asset's lifespan, the lower the required leverage (in the extreme case of 100 percent periodic capital consumption, as in inventories and receivables, the investment should be totally financed by a loan [$f = 1$]; by way of contrast, in the case of zero depreciation—as in land—equity finance will not lead to equity erosion [$f = 0$]); (3) the depreciation method, expressing the actual capital consumption, affects the required leverage. Accelerated depreciation would necessitate a higher break-even leverage relative to the straight-line method.

In the discrete case, where inflation is assumed to occur at the end of the year, the right-hand term in relation (7.14) should be restated as the following:

$$f = (1 + p)PV(D)_h \qquad (7.15)$$

For example, the present value of the depreciation charges on a $100 investment with a lifespan of 5 years, without a salvage value, and $h = 0.10$, under the straight-line depreciation method is $75.82, and under the sum-of-the-years-digits method—$80.60 (Shashua and Goldschmidt, 1983), pp. 183, 184). Suppose $p = 0.068$, then the required levels of financial leverage are 81 percent and 86 percent, respectively.

In conclusion, the longer the lifespan of the assets, the higher the inflation tax benefit, and vice versa. In respect to the inflation tax effect, assets can be classified into three groups: current assets (monetary assets and inventories), depreciable fixed assets, and nondepreciable fixed assets. For the inflation tax effect to be neutral, current assets should be financed fully by loans, whereas nondepreciable fixed assets can be financed totally by equity. Depreciable assets should be financed by a combination of equity and loans; the level of this combination depends on the level of inflation, the assets' lifespan, and the depreciation method used.

NOTES

1. This type of depreciation is easy to handle in the continuous case. Nevertheless, the results will hold for any other type of depreciation, as long as the return on the asset is equal to the discount rate (Morris, 1960, pp. 51–52).

2. Formulas for deriving the present value of depreciation schedules for various depreciation methods appear in the literature (e.g., Shashua and Goldschmidt, 1983, pp. 182–186).

EIGHT

ANALYSIS OF THE FINANCIAL POSITION OF THE UNITED STATES FARM SECTOR

In the preceding chapters the effect of inflation on the liquidity aspects and burden of loans has been shown analytically. In this chapter we try to determine to what extent the behavior of the United States farm sector is actually affected by past inflation. For this purpose, the loans, average interest rate, the interest costs, and the inflation-induced tax liability are analyzed.

The trend of the financial variables over the period 1950–1982 corresponds with the expectations expressed in the analytical models described earlier. The financial position of the sector during this period worsened considerably.[1]

8.1 THE LEVEL AND COMPOSITION OF DEBT, 1950–1982

One of the well-known trends in the financial situation of the United States farm sector is the significant increase in the volume of debt. This trend is accompanied by an increase in nominal interest rates, thus causing the volume of interest expenses to increase even more. The growth in outstanding debt and in annual interest expenses, in constant prices, is depicted in figure 8.1. The volume of debt increased, in constant prices, by more than four times in the analyzed period 1950–1982, and the volume of interest expenses increased more than nine-fold. In comparison, the value of gross receipts, in constant prices (inflated by the Consumer Price Index), increased relatively slightly—by roughly 50 percent in the same period. These trends imply a significant increase in the financial burden on the farm sector.

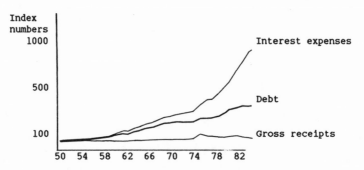

Fig. 8.1 Growth in debt and interest expenses,
in constant prices, U.S. farm sector

The rising trend in the volume of debt differed among the two types of loans, as can be seen in table 8.1. The volume of non-real estate debt, in constant prices, almost quadrupled in the 32-year period (from \$26.9 billion in January 1950 to \$102 billion in January 1983), whereas the volume of real estate debt increased by more than five times in the same period. The rate of growth in the volume of real estate loans was higher than that of non-real estate loans until 1970, at which time the trend in the rates of growth reversed. This situation is shown by the figures at the foot of table 8.1. The share

Table 8.1 Level of Debt, U.S. Farm Sector, Selected Years

	Jan. 1950	Jan. 1960	Jan. 1970	Jan. 1980	Jan. 1983	Increase 1983–1950	Growth 1983/1950
Billion dollars in January 1983 prices[a]							
Non-real estate debt	26.9	39.5	58.5	95.8	102.0	75.1	3.79
Real estate debt	19.5	35.2	67.6	98.2	100.8	81.3	5.17
Total debt	46.4	74.7	126.1	194.0	202.8	156.4	
Share of non-real estate debt (percent)	58	53	46	49	50		
Ratio of non-real estate debt to real estate debt	1.37	1.12	0.87	0.98	1.01		

[a]*Source:* Appendix table 10.C

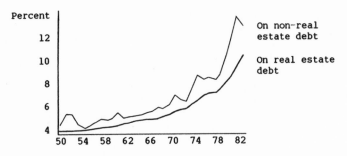

Fig. 8.2 Average interest rates,
U.S. farm sector (appendix table 8.A)

of non-real estate debt, which in 1950 was 58 percent of total debt, decreased to 46 percent in 1970 and then increased again to 50 percent. To put it another way, the ratio of non-real estate debt to real estate debt decreased from 1.37 in 1950 to 0.87 in 1970, and then increased to 1.01 in January 1983.

The trend of debts in the period 1950–1970 was beneficial to the farm sector because (1) the average interest rate on non-real estate debt is higher than that on real estate debt (figure 8.2), and (2) the repayment burden is lower. However, the switch in trends beginning from 1970 caused increasing financial burden on the sector, as shown in section 8.4. Projecting this trend suggests that the burden of the debt, on both principal repayments and interest payment, will increase in the future.

8.2 NOMINAL AND REAL INTEREST RATES, 1950–1982

The graphs in figure 8.1 indicate that interest payments increased, in constant prices, by more than twice as much as the volume of debt. This implies that nominal interest rates more than doubled during the analyzed period 1950–1982. To find the trend in interest rates, the actual rates must first be determined as shown below.

The actual interest rate on a stock of loans, where principal increments and decrements and interest payments take place many times throughout the year, is estimated by relation (3.15), which is restated here as follows:

$$r = \frac{2I}{L_{t-1} + L_t - I} \tag{8.1}$$

where r = effective annual interest rate,

     I = total interest expense on L,

    L = balance of loans.

Using relation (8.1), the effective interest rate on non-real estate debt for the United States farm sector in 1982 (appendix tables 8.C and 10.A) is estimated to be

$$r = \frac{2 \times 11.35}{91.5 + 102.0 - 11.35} = 0.1246 = 12.46\%$$

The inflation-free interest rate is calculated by

$$r^* = \frac{1 + r}{1 + p} - 1 = \frac{r - p}{1 + p} \tag{8.2}$$

where r* = inflation-free interest rate,

    r = actual interest rate,

    p = inflation rate.

The inflation-free interest rate on non-real estate debt for 1982 (the above example) is

$$r^* = \frac{1 + 0.1246}{1 + 0.0354} - 1 = 0.0861 = 8.61\%$$

The corresponding rate for 1979 is

$$r^* = \frac{1 + 0.1011}{1 + 0.1397} - 1 = -0.0339 = -3.39\%$$

The negative interest rate results from the fact that the inflation rate was higher than the nominal interest rate. Thus, in 1979, the borrower gained on each $1 of debt a sum of $0.0339, resulting from the reduction of the purchasing power of the outstanding debt.

    Relations (8.1) and (8.2) are used to determine the interest rates for the two groups of loans in the analyzed period. The results are depicted in figure 8.2 and the figures are presented in appendix table 8.A. Figure 8.2 shows that the average nominal interest rate on the non-real estate debt is higher than that on the real estate debt. The difference between these two rates increased considerably after 1979, because of the contracted nature of real estate loans. These are long-term loans and only the interest rate on new loans is affected by

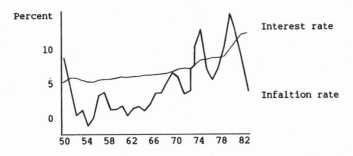

Fig. 8.3 Inflation and interest rates,
U.S. farm sector (appendix table 8.A)

inflation; whereas non-real estate loans are mainly short-term, with rates following the market's.

In the period 1950–1965, nominal interest rates were relatively stable (appendix table 8.A): 5–6 percent on non-real estate debt and 4.7–5.5 percent on real estate debt. After 1966, nominal interest rates rose steadily to about 13 percent and 10 percent (in 1982) on non-real estate debt and real estate debt, respectively.

In contrast to the smooth change of nominal rates, inflation-free rates fluctuated considerably, especially in the period 1973–1982 (appendix table 8.A). The behavior of inflation-free interest rates can be seen in figure 8.3, where the average interest rate on total debt is graphed alongside the inflation rate. In those years in which the inflation rate is higher than the interest rate, the inflation-free interest rate was negative. Thus, in one-half of the years during the period 1973–1982, the inflation-free interest rate was negative.

The average annual inflation-free interest rate on total debt was relatively stable during the period 1951–1972, and especially during the period 1956–1967, when the inflation rate was very low. The average inflation-free rate over the period 1951–1972 was 2.95 percent, while for the period 1973–1982 the rate was 0.30 percent (if 1982 is excluded, the average rate was −0.50 percent). The average rate during the 33 years was 2.14 percent on the total debt, 2.61 percent on the non-real estate debt, and 1.68 percent on the real estate debt (appendix table 8.A).

Inflation-free rates were negative in those years when the inflation rate was high, especially in 1950, 1973, 1974, and 1978–1980.[2] In other words, the level of real interest rates has been affected by inflation. Negative and low inflation-free rates indicate that the farm sector reaped windfall gains on its outstanding debt. These gains,

Table 8.2   Ratios of Financial Leverage, U.S. Farm Sector, Selected Years

	1950–51 (%)	960--61 (%)	1970–71 (%)	1980 (%)	1982 (%)	Growth 1982/ 1950–51
Total debt to total assets	11	13	18	17	19	1.73
Non-real estate debt to real estate assets	14	23	29	36	41	2.73
Total debt to assets excluding land	21	34	52	60	70	3.33
Total debt to gross receipts	34	61	88	117	128	3.80

Source: Appendix table 8.B.

however, almost vanished in 1982, except for such gains on the outstanding "old" loans.

8.3 TRENDS IN FINANCIAL LEVERAGE

Financial leverage is usually evaluated by the ratio of debt to total assets. In the case of the farm sector, however, this ratio provides only a limited amount of information because of changes in the value of land. The physical volume of land is more or less stable, but its value has changed significantly over the years. In order to enable analysts to make a meaningful time series comparison of the financial position of the farm sector (and also comparisons with other sectors of the economy), four ratios are used here: (1) total debt to total assets, (2) non-real estate debt to non-real estate assets, (3) total debt to assets excluding land,[3] and (4) total debt to gross receipts.[4] The ratio of debt to gross receipts, which is called the debt turnover ratio, is often used for evaluating the credit standing of a firm because this ratio measures debt relative to the firm's activity.

The four ratios measuring the financial leverage of the United States farm sector for selected years are presented in table 8.2; ratios for each year in the period 1950–1982 are presented in appendix table 8.B. The ratios of total debt to total assets show a relatively slight increase during the analyzed period 1950–1982 (from 11 percent to 19 percent). The other ratios increased much more, especially the ratios of debt to assets excluding land and debt to gross receipts; the latter ratio increased almost four-fold. The trend of three ratios

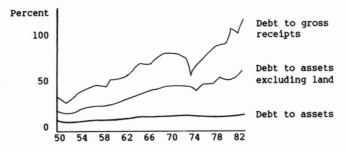

Fig. 8.4 Ratios of financial leverage,
U.S. farm sector (appendix table 8.B)

is depicted in figure 8.4. As can be seen, the trend in the latter two ratios is concurrent with the trend in the volume of debt, in constant prices, as shown in figure 8.1.

The graphs in figure 8.4 show that deterioration in the financial position of the United States farm sector accelerated considerably during the 1970s, when the inflation rate was high. The worsening in the financial position caused a financial burden as shown in the next section, which in turn implies additional increase in the financial leverage. The accelerated increase in the non-real estate debt relative to the real estate debt since 1970 (table 8.1) enlarges the financial burden in the farm sector because annual debt services of the former are higher.

Comparison with Other Sectors

A comparison of the financial leverage of the United States farm sector with other sectors is presented in table 8.3, using a different set of data (therefore producing ratios different from those in table 8.2). The ratio of total debt to total assets excluding land for the farm business surpassed that of the other two sectors in the early 1980s. It is interesting to note that the financial leverage of nonfinancial corporate business was relatively stable during the period (about 40 percent), because corporations increased their equity share by issuing shares to the public covering their needs for finance.

Financial Leverage by Farm Size

Table 8.4 lists the level of financial leverage by farm size. These figures represent the ratio of total debt to total assets excluding real

Table 8.3   Ratios of Financial Leverage, Three U.S. Sectors, Selected Years, Total Debt to Total Assets Excluding Land

| | Ratios (percent) | | | | | |
	Jan. 1950	Jan. 1960	Jan. 1970	Jan. 1980	Jan. 1983	Growth 1983/1950
Farm business	16	28	43	48	54	3.38
Nonfarm noncorporate business	9	16	30	41	41	4.56
Nonfinancial corporate business	38	42	48	41	41	1.08

Source: Board of Governors of the Federal Reserve System (1984). Assets are recorded in replacement values.

estate assets. The level of financial leverage increases with size: In the largest size group ($500,000 in sales and over) the financial leverage is extremely high—104 percent in January 1980 and 117 percent in January 1983, compared to 72 percent and 86 percent for all farms in these two years, respectively.

Estimates for distribution of financial leverage among different size groups of farms in the United States farm sector for 1984 have been published by Melichar (1984); some of these figures are reproduced in table 8.5. The first row in table 8.5 shows that in 8 percent of all farms, financial leverage (ratio of debt to assets) is over 71 percent and in 19 percent of farms, it is over 41 percent. In comparison, the second row shows that in 19 percent of the large-size group (over

Table 8.4   Ratios of Financial Leverage, Sales Classes, U.S. Farm Sector, Total Debt to Total Assets Excluding Real Estate

	Number of Farms (thousands)	Jan. 1980 (%)	Jan. 1983 (%)
All farms	2,430	72	86
Up to $39,999	1,755	58	68
$40,000 to $99,999	388	64	78
$100,000 to $199,999	179	72	86
$200,000 to $499,999	84	85	102
$500,000 and over	24	104	117

Source: USDA (1983), pp. 128, 131. Excluding farm households. The figures differ from those in table 8.2 because real estate includes land and structures. No data on structures were available.

Table 8.5   Distribution of Farms According to Three Categories of Financial Leverage, Sales Classes, U.S. Farm Sector, Estimates January 1984

| | Financial Leverage[a] (percent) | | | |
	Below 40	41-70	Over 71	Total
Number of farms in each category				
All farms (%)	81	11	8	100
Large farms (%)	56	25	19	100
Medium farms (%)	69	18	13	100
Total debt in each category				
All farms (%)	37	32	31	100

[a]Ratio of total debt to total assets.
Source: Melichar (1984), p. 9. Estimates, calculated by Melichar, based on data from the Bureau of the Census, *1979 Farm Finance Survey.* Large farms are with sales over $200,000, medium farms with sales $40,000–$199,999, in 1979 prices.

$200,000 of sales, comprising about 4.4 percent of all farms and producing about 50 percent of the total farm production), financial leverage is over 71 percent, and in 44 percent of these farms leverage is over 41 percent. On the other hand, 31 percent of the debt is held by farms with a financial leverage above 71 percent, as shown at the foot of table 8.5.

8.4 TRENDS IN THE INTEREST BILL

Financial burden results from interest expenses and loan repayments. In the case of the United States farm sector, only the burden resulting from the interest bill is analyzed here. The aspect of loan repayments is ignored because relevant data are not available, and it is assumed that the repaid loans can be replaced by new loans. (This assumption does not necessarily hold for a single farm.) It should be noted, however, that during inflation, new loans are usually granted at higher interest rates and shorter terms compared to the original loans, as actually happened in the United States farm sector (table 8.1 and figure 8.2).

The absolute financial burden in the United States farm sector, resulting only from the interest bill, increased by about nine times, in constant prices, during the analyzed period 1950–1982 (figure 8.1). Since interest expenses are paid from cash income, these two items should be compared. Interest expenses and cash income for the

Table 8.6   Interest Expenses and Cash Income, U.S. Farm Sector, 1950–1982 (billion dollars in 1982 prices)

| Year | Interest Expenses | | | Cash Income | | Ratio of Interest to Cash Before Interest |
	On Non-Real Estate Debt	On Real Estate Debt	Total	Before Interest	After Interest	
1950	0.90	1.34	2.24	50.82	48.59	0.04
1951	0.93	1.49	2.41	54.95	52.53	0.04
1952	0.98	1.64	2.62	52.08	49.46	0.05
1953	1.07	1.56	2.63	51.53	48.90	0.05
1954	1.14	1.51	2.65	46.62	43.97	0.06
1955	1.26	1.59	2.85	44.98	42.13	0.06
1956	1.37	1.66	3.03	47.00	43.96	0.06
1957	1.45	1.71	3.16	42.42	39.26	0.07
1958	1.51	1.88	3.39	47.72	44.33	0.07
1959	1.65	2.15	3.80	43.78	39.99	0.09
1960	1.79	2.34	4.13	45.36	41.23	0.09
1961	1.95	2.30	4.25	47.06	42.81	0.09
1962	2.13	2.58	4.71	47.31	42.60	0.10
1963	2.36	2.85	5.21	46.98	41.78	0.11
1964	2.63	2.98	5.60	48.28	42.68	0.12
1965	2.93	3.14	6.07	50.12	44.06	0.12
1966	3.18	3.39	6.57	56.40	49.82	0.12
1967	3.43	3.67	7.10	49.80	42.70	0.14
1968	3.67	3.65	7.32	50.60	43.28	0.14
1969	3.86	3.77	7.63	54.56	46.93	0.14
1970	3.94	4.02	7.95	53.28	45.32	0.15
1971	4.09	3.95	8.03	50.29	42.26	0.16
1972	4.30	4.15	8.45	61.71	53.26	0.14
1973	4.67	4.94	9.61	86.14	76.53	0.11
1974	5.01	5.60	10.61	77.44	66.83	0.14
1975	5.38	5.49	10.88	62.74	51.87	0.17
1976	5.82	6.05	11.87	61.51	49.64	0.19
1977	6.27	6.68	12.95	56.30	43.34	0.23
1978	6.83	7.64	14.46	68.15	53.69	0.21
1979	7.51	9.10	16.62	67.49	50.88	0.25
1980	8.09	10.19	18.27	62.21	43.94	0.29
1981	8.90	11.36	20.26	54.81	34.55	0.37
1982	9.63	11.35	20.98	48.90	27.92	0.43

Source: Appendix table 8.C.

analyzed period are presented in table 8.6, in constant prices (using the year's average Consumer Price Index; appendix table 11.E), and in appendix table 8.C, in nominal prices. The figures in table 8.6 show that while the cash income before interest is more or less constant, with some fluctuations, throughout the period, the volume

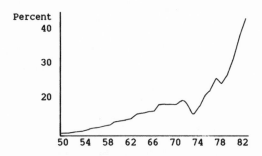

Fig. 8.5 Ratio of interest to cash income
before interest, U.S. farm sector (table 8.6)

of interest expenses increased considerably. Thus, the ratio of interest expenses to cash income before interest rose considerably—from about 4 percent in the early 1950s to about 40 percent in the early 1980s. This trend is shown in figure 8.5.

It is interesting to note that the ratio of interest expense to cash income before interest doubled within the last five years of the analyzed period—from about 20 percent in the years 1975–1978 to 43 percent in 1982. Projecting this trend by extrapolation implies that the burden of interest payments would become unbearable in the future.

Figures on cash income are usually less available than figures on sales or gross receipts, especially on the firm level. Therefore, it is customary in business to relate expense items and net income to sales. Thus, the following three ratios have been calculated for the farm sector: (1) operating income to gross receipts, (2) interest expense to gross receipts, and (3) cash receipts before and after interest to gross receipts. The resulting ratios for the period 1950–1982 are presented in appendix table 8.D and are depicted in figure 8.6.

Figure 8.6 shows that the ratio of total interest expense to gross receipts increased from about 2 percent in the early 1950s to about 14 percent in 1982, whereas the ratios of operating income (section 10.2) and cash income to gross receipts were more or less constant during the period, except for a slight decline in the latter ratio in the last ten years. Out of one dollar of gross receipts, about one-third ($0.30 to $0.40) is left as cash income before paying interest. Of this cash income, $0.02 was paid out as interest in the early 1950s and $0.14 in 1982. The balance of cash is left for consumption and investments—for asset replacement and capital formation. With the

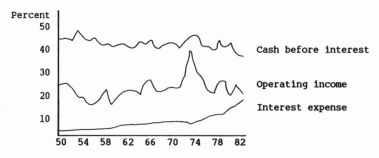

Fig. 8.6 Cash flow ratios related to gross
receipts, U.S. farm sector (appendix table 8.D)

shrinking of this cash residual, the level of investment has declined, as is shown in section 11.4.

In summary, as long as the interest expense was only a small share of the cash income, which was the situation in the United States farm sector until the late 1970s, the financial burden was unnoticed. But the steeply rising trend in financial leverage and nominal interest rates increased the loans' interest and repayments on principal beyond the capability of farm income. This situation forced farmers to seek more loans, thus—typically in a period of inflation—accelerating this process. Projecting the trend shown in figure 8.6 implies heavy financial stress in the farm sector, especially in high leveraged farms.

It is interesting to note that financial burden differs not only among size groups (tables 8.4 and 8.5) but also by type of farm, as shown in table 8.7, which gives a sample of farms in the upper Midwest. The figures at the top of table 8.7 indicate that financial leverage, as measured by the ratio of debt to gross income, increased. Especially was this true in beef farms, where leverage increased by about 50 percent from 1979 to 1981. The ratio of interest expense to gross income increased by much more (foot of table 8.7)—by 60 to 70 percent in dairy and cash crop farms, and by 160 percent in beef farms.

8.5 INFLATION AND TAX LIABILITIES, 1960–1974

The discussion in chapter 7 indicates that during inflation the prevailing income tax regulations caused the phenomenon of equity erosion on the one hand, and of tax rebate on loans, on the other. The difference between the two effects represents the net equity erosion.

Table 8.7   Financial Leverage and Interest Bill, Groups of Farms by Type, Upper Midwest, Ratios and Growth, 1979–1981

	Type of Farm				
	Dairy		Cash Crop North		Beef North
Location	Wisconsin		Dakota		Dakota
Number of observations[a]	2100		700		75
Debt to gross income					
1979(%)	142		189		201
1981 (%)	173		206		299
1981–1979		1.22		1.09	1.49
Interest expense to gross income					
1979(%)	10.7		11.7		12.4
1981(%)	17.4		20.4		32.1
1981–1979		1.62		1.74	2.60

[a]Rounded average over 1979–1981.
Source: Thompson (1983), pp. 466–67. Farms which tend to be large, growing, and more highly leveraged than average farms.

To estimate the net inflation tax effect, tax liabilities resulting from depreciation and from interest expenses must first be determined. This is carried out by relation (7.2), which is reproduced here:

$$\text{Net change in tax liability} = (D_h - D_c) - (I_r - I_a) \quad (8.3)$$

where D_h, D_c = depreciation charges, historical and current, respectively,

I_r, I_a = interest expenses, real and actual, respectively.

The first term in relation (8.3) represents the difference in tax liability due to depreciation, whereas the second represents the difference in tax liability due to interest.

To estimate tax liabilities resulting from inflation tax effects in the United States farm sector, data on historical depreciation are needed. Using available data for the period 1960–1974, the net tax liability of the farm sector has been measured by applying relation (8.3). The relevant data and the resulting figures for net tax liability are presented in appendix table 8.E. The figures show that, in all years, net tax liabilities resulting from inflation were negative. In other words, in every year between 1960 and 1974, the farm sector was slightly overtaxed by the corresponding net tax liability multiplied by the relevant income tax rate.

The level of net tax liabilities resulting from inflation in constant prices declined over the period 1960–1973. One can surmise that this declining tendency continued after 1973 because of the significant increase in financial leverage in that period.

NOTES

1. It should be mentioned that the cash flow problem in agriculture due to the effect of inflation was explored, theoretically and empirically, by Tweeten (1981a, 1981b).

2. Negative and low inflation-free rates are caused by two factors: (1) a lag in the adjustment of market interest rates to inflation, especially when inflation is not persistent (for evidence on negative interest rates see, e.g., Leuthold, 1981); and (2) the outstanding debt balance includes loans taken when interest rates were low.

3. In the case of the United States farm sector, a significant volume of loans are taken out to finance land, because land provides an excellent collateral for loans.

4. Given that gross receipts are recorded in the year's average prices, the balance of debt at the beginning of the year was multiplied by $(1 + p/2)$, where p is the year's inflation rate (see section 11.1).

APPENDIX

Table 8.A   Average Interest Rates, U.S. Farm Sector, 1950–1982

Year	Inflation Rate	Nominal Rates			Inflation-Free Rates		
		Non-Real Estate Debt	Real Estate Debt	All Debt	Non-Real Estate Debt	Real Estate Debt	All Debt
1950	7.94	5.27	4.65	5.00	−2.47	−3.05	−2.72
1951	4.20	5.94	4.69	5.39	1.67	0.47	1.14
1952	0.63	5.93	4.66	5.38	5.26	4.00	4.72
1953	1.13	5.21	4.75	5.02	4.04	3.58	3.84
1954	−0.74	4.89	4.77	4.84	5.68	5.55	5.62
1955	0.25	5.01	4.80	4.91	4.74	4.54	4.65
1956	3.11	5.32	4.86	5.10	2.14	1.70	1.93
1957	3.50	5.61	4.97	5.29	2.03	1.41	1.73
1958	1.28	5.48	4.95	5.23	4.14	3.62	3.90
1959	1.27	5.64	5.03	5.36	4.32	3.72	4.04
1960	1.59	6.07	5.14	5.63	4.41	3.49	3.98
1961	0.67	5.63	5.27	5.46	4.92	4.57	4.75
1962	1.33	5.76	5.35	5.56	4.37	3.96	4.17
1963	1.65	5.86	5.44	5.66	4.14	3.73	3.95
1964	1.08	5.91	5.48	5.70	4.77	4.35	4.57
1965	1.92	6.02	5.51	5.76	4.02	3.52	3.77
1966	3.35	6.20	5.56	5.87	2.75	2.14	2.44
1967	3.45	6.45	5.65	6.03	2.90	2.13	2.50
1968	4.61	6.35	5.76	6.04	1.67	1.11	1.37
1969	6.19	6.66	5.94	6.27	0.45	−0.23	0.08
1970	5.21	7.32	6.10	6.66	2.01	0.85	1.38
1971	3.36	6.96	6.27	6.59	3.49	2.82	3.13
1972	3.65	6.81	6.33	6.56	3.05	2.58	2.80
1973	9.40	7.79	6.60	7.16	−1.47	−2.56	−2.05
1974	11.74	8.85	6.95	7.84	−2.58	−4.28	−3.49
1975	6.79	8.50	7.28	7.85	1.60	0.46	0.99
1976	5.16	8.62	7.48	8.02	3.29	2.21	2.72
1977	6.73	8.47	7.57	8.01	1.63	0.79	1.20
1978	9.41	8.76	7.79	8.27	−0.60	−1.47	−1.04
1979	13.97	10.11	8.20	9.15	−3.39	−5.06	−4.23
1980	11.74	11.62	8.69	10.11	−0.11	−2.73	−1.46
1981	8.21	13.15	9.52	11.27	4.57	1.22	2.83
1982	3.54	12.46	10.24	11.33	8.61	6.46	7.52
Average	4.46	7.11	6.13	6.62	2.61	1.68	2.14

Note: Interest rates derived from the actual interest expenses.

Appendix Table 8.B   Ratios of Financial Leverage, U.S. Farm Sector, 1950–1982

Year	Total[a]	Debt to Assets Non-Real Estate[b]	Excluding Land[c]	Debt to Gross Receipts
1950	10.59	16.09	21.92	36.50
1951	9.55	13.95	19.86	32.29
1952	9.63	14.12	19.94	36.20
1953	10.84	17.08	23.35	44.32
1954	11.73	18.79	25.76	46.62
1955	11.93	19.18	26.76	50.06
1956	12.34	20.31	28.86	53.12
1957	11.89	19.18	28.71	53.33
1958	11.92	19.30	29.07	49.65
1959	12.63	21.11	30.20	59.93
1960	13.01	22.62	33.04	61.13
1961	13.62	23.63	35.00	61.87
1962	14.18	24.73	36.79	64.54
1963	15.08	26.70	39.48	70.06
1964	15.87	28.95	43.13	78.73
1965	16.40	30.07	46.48	76.80
1966	16.79	29.80	47.51	78.64
1967	17.24	30.31	48.91	85.62
1968	17.68	31.30	51.11	90.66
1969	17.89	30.53	51.67	89.44
1970	18.08	29.71	51.86	89.92
1971	18.02	29.28	52.12	87.18
1972	18.25	30.22	52.57	83.18
1973	17.63	28.56	50.25	66.28
1974	16.26	26.50	46.74	77.03
1975	17.15	30.67	53.91	82.15
1976	16.68	30.96	54.00	90.09
1977	16.39	33.94	57.01	98.48
1978	17.46	38.06	62.24	100.67
1979	16.79	36.13	59.06	99.76
1980	17.04	35.78	60.25	117.62
1981	17.24	36.79	62.85	114.16
1982	19.24	40.67	69.71	128.37
1983		43.33	73.03	

[a]Total debt to total assets.
[b]Non-real estate debt to non-real estate assets.
[c]Total debt to total assets excluding land.

Appendix Table 8.C   Interest Expenses and Cash Income, U.S. Farm Sector, 1950–1982 (billion dollars in nominal prices)

| Year | Interest Expenses | | | Cash Income | |
	On Non-Real Estate Debt	On Real Estate Debt	Total	Before Interest	After Interest
1950	0.33	0.23	0.56	12.70	12.14
1951	0.40	0.25	0.65	14.81	14.16
1952	0.45	0.27	0.72	14.35	13.62
1953	0.43	0.30	0.73	14.30	13.57
1954	0.42	0.32	0.74	13.01	12.27
1955	0.44	0.35	0.79	12.50	11.71
1956	0.47	0.39	0.86	13.26	12.40
1957	0.50	0.42	0.92	12.39	11.47
1958	0.57	0.45	1.02	14.32	13.30
1959	0.65	0.50	1.15	13.24	12.10
1960	0.72	0.55	1.27	13.94	12.67
1961	0.71	0.61	1.32	14.61	13.29
1962	0.81	0.67	1.48	14.85	13.37
1963	0.91	0.75	1.65	14.93	13.27
1964	0.96	0.85	1.80	15.54	13.74
1965	1.03	0.96	1.99	16.41	14.43
1966	1.14	1.07	2.21	18.99	16.78
1967	1.27	1.19	2.46	17.25	14.79
1968	1.32	1.33	2.64	18.27	15.63
1969	1.43	1.47	2.90	20.76	17.86
1970	1.62	1.59	3.20	21.47	18.27
1971	1.66	1.72	3.38	21.14	17.76
1972	1.80	1.87	3.67	26.79	23.13
1973	2.28	2.16	4.43	39.73	35.30
1974	2.87	2.56	5.43	39.63	34.20
1975	3.07	3.01	6.08	35.05	28.97
1976	3.57	3.44	7.01	36.34	29.33
1977	4.20	3.94	8.15	35.40	27.26
1978	5.17	4.62	9.79	46.12	36.33
1979	6.87	5.67	12.53	50.91	38.38
1980	8.72	6.92	15.64	53.24	37.61
1981	10.72	8.40	19.12	51.72	32.60
1982	11.35	9.63	20.98	48.90	27.92

Source: USDA (1983), pp. 15, 18.

Appendix Table 8.D   Cash Flow Ratios, U.S. Farm Sector, 1950–1982

Year	Inflation Rate	Operating Income to Gross Receipts	Interest Expense to Gross Receipts	Cash Income to Gross Receipts Before Interest	Cash Income to Gross Receipts After Interest	Debt to Gross Receipts
1950	7.94	20.85	1.75	39.80	38.05	36.50
1951	4.20	21.75	1.76	40.03	38.27	32.29
1952	0.63	19.18	1.99	39.52	37.53	36.20
1953	1.13	15.28	2.22	43.47	41.26	44.32
1954	−0.74	15.42	2.26	39.77	37.51	46.62
1955	0.25	13.16	2.47	39.06	36.59	50.06
1956	3.11	13.51	2.63	40.79	38.15	53.12
1957	3.50	14.16	2.78	37.33	34.55	53.33
1958	1.28	19.01	2.73	38.39	35.66	49.65
1959	1.27	12.59	3.18	36.69	33.51	59.93
1960	1.59	15.79	3.42	37.58	34.16	61.13
1961	0.67	17.82	3.42	37.85	34.43	61.87
1962	1.33	18.46	3.66	36.76	33.10	64.54
1963	1.65	18.03	4.00	36.15	32.14	70.06
1964	1.08	16.50	4.50	38.76	34.26	78.73
1965	1.92	22.23	4.48	37.05	32.56	76.80
1966	3.35	22.82	4.60	39.49	34.89	78.64
1967	3.45	18.39	5.13	35.95	30.82	85.62
1968	4.61	17.81	5.37	37.14	31.76	90.66
1969	6.19	19.84	5.41	38.73	33.31	89.44
1970	5.21	19.73	5.74	38.47	32.73	89.92
1971	3.36	19.37	5.73	35.89	30.16	87.18
1972	3.65	25.07	5.42	39.57	34.16	83.18
1973	9.40	34.40	4.66	41.78	37.11	66.28
1974	11.74	26.33	5.80	42.34	36.54	77.03
1975	6.79	24.73	6.37	36.74	30.37	82.15
1976	5.16	19.05	7.24	37.50	30.27	90.09
1977	6.73	17.46	8.02	34.85	26.83	98.48
1978	9.41	22.14	8.20	38.66	30.46	100.67
1979	13.97	22.50	8.88	36.06	27.18	99.76
1980	11.74	16.13	11.22	38.19	26.98	117.62
1981	8.21	20.43	12.32	33.32	21.00	114.16
1982	3.54	17.50	14.03	32.69	18.66	128.37

Appendix Table 8.E   Tax Liabilities Resulting from Inflation Tax Effects, U.S. Farm Sector, 1960–1974 (billion dollars–nominal prices)

Year	Depreciation[a]			Interest[b]			Net Tax Liability[c]
	Historical	Current	Difference	Actual	Imputed	Difference	
1960	3.12	4.34	(1.22)	1.27	0.90	0.37	(0.85)
1961	3.14	4.39	(1.25)	1.32	0.90	0.42	(0.83)
1962	3.24	4.53	(1.29)	1.48	1.00	0.48	(0.81)
1963	3.34	4.70	(1.36)	1.65	1.10	0.55	(0.81)
1964	3.45	4.90	(1.46)	1.80	1.15	0.65	(0.81)
1965	3.58	5.11	(1.53)	1.99	1.26	0.73	(0.80)
1966	3.76	5.38	(1.63)	2.21	1.35	0.86	(0.77)
1967	4.02	5.78	(1.76)	2.46	1.54	0.92	(0.84)
1968	4.29	6.20	(1.91)	2.64	1.67	0.97	(0.94)
1969	4.51	6.57	(2.06)	2.90	1.78	1.12	(0.94)
1970	4.78	6.76	(1.98)	3.20	1.95	1.25	(0.73)
1971	5.24	7.35	(2.11)	3.38	2.15	1.35	(0.76)
1972	5.48	7.89	(2.40)	3.67	2.03	1.52	(0.88)
1973	6.08	8.94	(2.86)	4.43	2.43	2.00	(0.86)
1974	6.84	10.64	(3.80)	5.43	2.92	2.51	(1.29)

[a]*Source:* USDA (1976), p. 23.
[b]*Source:* Appendix tables 8.C and 10.F.
[c]Difference between depreciation charges and interest charges.

109

PART THREE

INCOME AND PERFORMANCE MEASUREMENT UNDER INFLATION

NINE

A MODEL FOR
INCOME MEASUREMENT FOR
A FARM SECTOR

Inflation affects a firm's reported income in two opposite directions. One effect is that the recorded values of assets (fixed and current) and the derived costs (depreciation and purchased inputs) are understated, because these are recorded at historical costs. The other effect is that the interest expenses include a premium or inflation-compensation for the decline in the purchasing power of the loan's principal. This premium is, as a matter of fact, a principal repayment but it is recorded as a cost, causing costs to be overstated.

The total real income figure includes some items—namely adjustments of values from the balance sheet—which are not under the control of the firm or sector for which income is measured and also are not realized during the accounting year. To arrive at an income measure that can be used for performance evaluation, noncontrollable items should be reported separately. Thus, total income is broken down into operating income, which has a meaning similar to the pre-inflation net income figure, and capital gains, which result from price-level impacts on balance sheet items.

For calculating operating income, nominal interest expenses, which represent the service of debt, must be adjusted so as to align with the adjustment of the costs representing the services realized from the assets. Thus, charging depreciation at real values (on revalued fixed assets) implies charging real or inflation-adjusted interest on loans that finance fixed assets. A similar procedure can be applied to costs related to current assets (purchased inputs) and interest on the corresponding loans, by adjusting both costs and interest expense.

However, this procedure involves adjustments of large amounts of data (periodical purchases) which usually are not available. Therefore, we propose to refrain from these adjustments, and instead, to charge nominal interest on working capital in conjunction with the charges of actual historical costs of purchased inputs.

The model for measuring income which is developed in this chapter assumes that there are no additions of equity and/or withdrawals of income during the year. (This assumption may hold for a sector but not necessarily for a firm.) The treatment of such transactions is presented in the appendix to the chapter.

The proposed model provides similar estimates of total income as measured by other models used in the United States (USDA, 1983; FASB, 1979) but differs significantly in breaking down total income into operating income and capital gains.

9.1 A MODEL FOR MEASURING TOTAL INCOME DURING INFLATION

The real income of a sector or a firm, in the economic sense, is determined by adding to the income that is reported by the conventional income statement some inflation adjustments of values related to balance sheet items, assuming no additions or withdrawals of equity. One possible procedure is to add to the net income the nominal changes in assets' value and to deduct the amount needed to maintain the purchasing power of equity; that is,

$$R = [SALES - PURS - DEPR - INTR + d\ INVY]$$
$$+ [d\ FIXA - p\ EQTY_{t-1}] \tag{9.1}$$

$$
\begin{aligned}
\text{where } R &= \text{real income} \\
PURS &= \text{purchased inputs, recorded value,} \\
DEPR &= \text{depreciation on current replacement cost of} \\
&\quad\ \text{assets, at year-end prices,} \\
INTR &= \text{interest on debt,} \\
INVY &= \text{inventories at current replacement value,} \\
FIXA &= \text{fixed assets, depreciated current replacement} \\
&\quad\ \text{value,} \\
EQTY &= \text{equity,} \\
t, t-1 &= \text{date of closing and opening balance sheets,} \\
&\quad\ \text{respectively,} \\
p &= \text{inflation rate between } t-1 \text{ and } t, \\
d\ INVY &= INVY_t - INVY_{t-1},
\end{aligned}
$$

| | = | nominal change in current replacement value of inventories, including physical change and price level gain, |

dFIXA $=$ FIXA$_t$ $-$ FIXA$_{t-1}$ $-$ Net investment,
$=$ nominal appreciation of fixed assets,

Net investment $=$ gross investment in fixed assets less depreciation on current replacement cost of assets, the latter stated in year-end prices,

p EQTY$_{t-1}$ $=$ equity maintenance $=$ amount required for maintaining the purchasing power of the equity.

The first bracketed part of relation (9.1) represents the conventional income statement where the change in the value of inventories, d INVY, is included in the cost of goods sold. The second bracketed part in relation (9.1) represents the adjustments of balance sheet items, assuming that the value of the financial assets is not affected by price level changes.

The meaning of relation (9.1) is that the real income in a given period amounts to the difference between sales and total costs (including purchased inputs, depreciation, imputed cost of operators' labor, interest, and the change in the recorded value of inventories) plus the nominal increase in the value of fixed assets, less the amount required for maintaining the purchasing power of the equity. This income is generated during the period under analysis and is stated in terms of end-of-period prices.

9.2 ILLUSTRATIVE EXAMPLES

Two simple examples, where the results are self-evident, are presented and used for applying the various procedures for income measurement. The first example illustrates a case of fixed assets (land); the second, a case of current assets (inventories). To simplify the presentation, it is assumed that in each illustrative firm there is only one type of asset, that there are no operating costs, and that there is no income tax.

Example of a Landowner

Consider a landowner with the following opening balance sheet, recorded at current replacement values: land $1,000, loan $500, equity $500. There are no principal repayments on the loan during the analyzed period. Under conditions of price stability, the interest on the loan, at the annual rate of 5 percent, is paid at the end of the year. The income from the land's rental, before interest expenses, is $100, received at the end of the year. During the year, neither the general price level nor the land prices changed. The resulting income is:

Income (rent)	$100
Less: Interest ($500 × 5%)	(25)
Net income	75

Consider now the same case under inflationary conditions, where both the general price level and land prices increased during the year by 20 percent. Under these conditions, the land's rental is $120 (instead of $100) and the interest on the loan is 26 percent (5 percent, inflation-compensated).

The conventional income statement at the end of the year is:

Income (rent)	$120
Less: interest ($500 × 26%)	130
Net income (loss)	(10)

The loss of $10, which equals the cash deficit, results from the fact that the interest expense of $130 (based on 26 percent) includes $100 (20 percent on the $500 loan) compensation for the decline in the purchasing power of the loan. This compensation is neither a gain nor a loss in the economic sense because it is offset by the land appreciation.

Applying relation (9.1), the real income is

$$R = [(120 - 130)] + [(1,200 - 1,000) - (0.20 \times 500)] = \$90$$

Assume now that the price of land increased by 25 percent, whereas the general price level increased, as assumed earlier, by 20 percent. Then, the real income is

$$R = [(120 - 130)] + [(1,250 - 1,000) - (0.20 \times 500)] = \$140$$

Example of a Salesman

Consider a salesman who purchases and sells 1,000 units of goods at the beginning of each quarter, and keeps a stable stock of inventory consisting of 1,000 units. To simplify the presentation, it is assumed that the selling price at each date of sale equals the purchasing price at this date. The price level of the goods increases at a constant rate of about 4.7 percent per quarter, which means a 20 percent increase during the year. The selling and purchasing price at the beginning of the year is $1 per unit. During the year, goods are sold for $4,300 and inputs are purchased for the same amount. The historical value of the opening inventory is $950, as it was acquired at the beginning of the last year's quarter, but its current value is $1,000.

The salesman finances his operations solely by loans. To simplify the presentation, the interest on the loan is set at the anticipated price level change (20 percent per annum)—that is, at zero real interest rate—and is paid only at the end of the year. The opening inventory is financed by a $950 loan on which there are no principal repayments during the analyzed period. As there is no extra cash, the salesman takes out a new loan to pay the $190 interest at the end of the year. Thus, the closing balance of inventory, which was acquired for $1,140, is financed by two loans totaling $1,140 (950 + 190).

The current-cost balance sheets are as follows:

	Opening	Closing	Change
Inventories, current cost	$1,000	$1,200	$200
Loans	(950)	(1,140)	(190)
Equity	50	60	10

The $10 increase in equity is 20 percent of the opening value, which provides equity maintenance. Applying relation (9.1), the real income is

$$R = (4,300 - 4,300 - 190) + (1,200 - 1,000)$$
$$- (0.20 \times 50) = \$0$$

9.3 THE ROLE OF INTEREST IN MEASURING OPERATING INCOME

The total income, as measured by relation (9.1), includes inflation adjustments of balance sheet items which are not under the control of the firm or sector for which the income is measured and also are not realized during the accounting year. Therefore, it is customary to report, as a separate figure, the portion of income that is similar in meaning to the pre-inflation net income, which does not include adjustments of balance sheet items. This figure, called operating income, is used for performance evaluation.

It is customary to inflation-adjust or revalue historical cost items that are derived from assets. On the other hand, interest on the loans that finance assets is usually not inflation-adjusted, despite the fact that interest expenses include principal repayment through the premium component in the nominal interest rate. This inconsistent practice causes reported operating income to be understated, as is illustrated in section 9.1, with two models which are presently used in the United States.

The USDA Economic Research Service (ERS) model for measuring real income (USDA, 1983—as shown in chapter 10) partitions total income into "residual income to equity" and "real capital gains." Residual income to equity for the landowner in section 9.2, after charging all interest expenses, will be −$10, although the correct figure is $90. The Financial Accounting Standards Board (1979) partitions total income into three components. The first component, called "income from continuing operations," is calculated after charging interest expenses, revalued depreciation and revalued cost of goods sold.[1] The calculated income from continuing operations for the salesman in section 9.2 will be −$190 instead of zero. (The correct calculations are presented below.)

To be consistent, interest expense, which represents debt service, should be treated in the same way as costs representing the services of assets. The question is, which costs and expenses—related to balance sheet items—should be charged in real (inflation-adjusted) terms and which costs and expenses should not be adjusted?

During a period of inflation, the decline in the purchasing power of loans is usually compensated by the inflationary element in nominal interest expenses. Because nominal interest expenses are considered as cost in the conventional income statement, the inflationary element in nominal interest can be deducted from interest expenses or can be added to conventional net income in calculating operating income.[2]

To put it differently, suppose the nominal interest rate during inflation is r and the pre-inflation interest rate is r*; if r follows the Fisher hypothesis, under the continuous case, then,

$$r = r^* + p$$

or, under the discrete case,

$$r = (1 + r^*)(1 + p) - 1 = r^*(1 + p) + p$$

where r = market, nominal interest rate,
  r* = real, inflation-free interest rate,
  p = inflation rate.

Consider a firm that holds only fixed assets, where the volume of the assets and outstanding debt do not change, in real terms, during the year. Then, the actual interest expense is:

$$INTR = r\ DEBT_{t-1} = r^*(1 + p)\ DEBT_{t-1} + p\ DEBT_{t-1}$$

where r = average actual interest rate.

The corresponding inflation-free interest expense is:

$$r^*(1 + p)\ DEBT_{t-1} = INTR - p\ DEBT_{t-1}$$

Let $r^*(1 + p)\ DEBT_{t-1} = I_F$. Then, relation (9.1) will take the following form:

$$R = [SALES - PURS - DEPR - I_F]$$
$$+ [(d\ FIXA - p\ EQTY_{t-1}) - (INTR - I_F)] \qquad (9.2)$$

It should be noted that the term $(INTR - I_F)$ represents the actual inflation-compensation on the debt. When the interest rate is fully inflation-compensated, then

$$INTR - I_F = p\ DEBT_{t-1}$$

Given that relation (9.2) is devised for a firm that holds only fixed assets, the first bracketed part of the relation represents the operating income and the second bracketed part represents the capital gains.

Applying relation (9.2) to the example of the landowner in section 9.2, provides the following results:

$$I_F = 0.05(1 + 0.20)\ 500 = \$30$$

For the case in which land value increases by the inflation rate,

$$R = [120 - 30] + [(1,200 - 1,000) - (0.20 \times 500)$$
$$- (130 - 30)] = \$90$$

For the case in which land value increases by 25 percent,

$$R = [120 - 30] + [(1,250 - 1,000) - (0.20 \times 500)$$
$$- (130 - 30)] = 90 + 50 = \$140$$

In both cases, operating income is $90, which is 20 percent above the pre-inflation income of $75, and the inflation-free interest expense is $30. Capital gains are zero in the first case and $50 in the second.

The discussion in chapters 1, 2, and 3 shows that during inflation, actual interest expenses on loans that finance working capital complement the historical cost of purchased inputs. Thus, actual costs of inputs and actual interest expenses on loans that finance working capital should be used in costing and in income measurement. This point is further analyzed below.

Consider a firm that holds only current assets financed fully by loans. In this case, relation (9.1) takes the following form:

$$R = [SALES - PURS - INTR + d\ INVY] - P\ EQTY \qquad (9.3)$$

Applying relation (9.3) to the example of the salesman in section 9.2, provides the following income:

$$R = [4,300 - 4,300 - 190 + (1,200 - 1,000)]$$
$$- (0.20 \times 50) = 10 - 10 = \$0$$

In conclusion, the following costing procedure should be used in measuring operating income: Actual interest on loans that finance current assets (assuming the assets are fully financed by loans) should be charged in conjunction with historical costs of purchased inputs. Real or inflation-free interest on loans that finance fixed assets should be charged in conjunction with revalued depreciation.

9.4 DETERMINING OPERATING INCOME

In a period of inflation it is important to find the sources of real total income. The accepted approach is to differentiate between operating income and gains on balance sheet items. The first income component is of special interest because it is viewed as an inflation-adjusted accrued net income figure, which conveys the same information as pre-inflation net income. It is therefore vital that operating income be calculated correctly, even if some variables must be estimated rather than measured accurately.

To measure operating income, the costs derived from two basic types of assets—fixed assets and current assets—plus the interest on loans that finance these two groups of assets, should be treated in a different way, as shown in the preceding section. For this purpose, the relevant individual components, in both the balance sheet and income statement, must be differentiated. In some cases, however, the differentiation is not straightforward, especially in the case of interest expenses.

The distinction between fixed assets and current assets is not always clear. Current assets are realized during the accounting year and appear in the income statement. For example, inventories appear as historical cost of goods sold and receivables appear as sales. Fixed assets, on the other hand, provide services over more than one accounting year, and their real value is usually maintained in a period of inflation. Financial assets such as investments, shares, and bonds can be classified separately or included in either of the two former categories. For simplicity, we include short-term financial assets within current assets, and long-term financial assets within fixed assets.

Current assets are usually financed by short-term and medium-term loans, whereas fixed assets are usually financed by long-term loans and equity.[3] Accordingly, a scheme of a typical balance sheet can be depicted as follows:

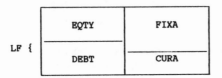

where FIXA = fixed assets and long-term financial assets
    CURA = current assets = inventories and financial assets that are realized during the accounting year,
        LF = FIXA − EQTY
            = DEBT − CURA
            = loans financing fixed assets.

The cost and interest variables in the income statement (the first four terms in relation [9.1]) should be differentiated into items that are related to either current assets or fixed assets, as follows:

$$OI = SALES - PURS - DEPR - I_C - I_F$$
$$+ \text{d INVY} \qquad (9.4)$$

where OI = operating income,
    I_C = interest expense on current assets, mainly on working capital,
    I_F = interest on loans financing fixed assets.

Determining Interest Charges

The main problem in measuring operating income concerns the estimation of the two categories of interest expenses. Following the discussion in the preceding section, interest on the loans that finance fixed assets is determined by

$$I_F = r^*(1 + p) LF \qquad (9.5)$$

where r^* = inflation-free interest rate.

The interest on current assets can be estimated by using one of the methods devised in chapter 3. The implications of using these methods should be considered. First, the actual average rate of interest on the relevant loans (usually short-term loans) is used as an imputed rate which is applied to working capital. This means that when current assets are financed partially by equity, the average interest on the loans is imputed to the corresponding equity. This procedure of applying imputed interest rates to all the capital that finances current assets makes it possible to do two things: match the nominal interest charges with historical values of purchase inputs and sales, and carry time series comparisons of operating income figures for performance evaluation.

The procedure of computing interest on working capital as proposed above may affect the level of depreciation charges. For example, suppose the cash surplus is allocated to finance the investments that are carried out during the year, where the level of investment equals asset replacement needs, which in turn is estimated by depreciation at replacement value. Then, assuming that the investment is evenly distributed over the year in constant prices, the nominal amount of investment with the interest thereon is approximately[4]

$$INVS_t = INVS (1 + r/2) = DEPR_t \tag{9.6}$$

where
$$\begin{aligned}
INVS_t &= \text{investment stated in year-end prices,} \\
INVS &= \text{investment at nominal value,} \\
r &= \text{interest rate on short-term loans,} \\
DEPR_t &= \text{depreciation at year-end prices.}
\end{aligned}$$

To prevent double counting of the interest charges, depreciation in this case should be stated in year's average prices, that is,

$$DEPR = DEPR_t/(1 + r/2) \tag{9.7}$$

The use of depreciation charges which are stated in year's average prices is compatible with the other items in the income statement, such as sales and purchases, which are recorded in year's average prices.

The interest expenses I_C and I_F are imputed charges, which differ from the actual interest expenses, INTR. The diference is made up of inflation-compensation on the loans financing fixed assets, and the difference between the actual interest on funds financing current assets and the imputed charges. Therefore, the difference between the actual interest expenses and the imputed charges

$$INTR - I_C - I_F \qquad (9.8)$$

should be considered as capital gains, as shown below.

9.5 CAPITAL GAINS AND HOLDING GAINS

The difference between total income, as measured by relation (9.1), and operating income, as measured by relation (9.4), represents capital gains. Capital gains include the second bracketed part of relation (9.1), which represents nominal appreciation on fixed assets less inflation-compensation on equity, minus relation (9.8) representing inflation-compensation on loans financing fixed assets and some additional minor sums. These gains usually are not under the control of the firm or sector for which income is measured.

Subtracting operating income—relation (9.4)—from total income— relation (9.1)—provides the capital gains, which should be attributed to equity. Thus capital gains are equal to

$$CG = d\ FIXA - P\ EQTY_{t-1} - (INTR - I_C - I_F) \quad (9.9)$$

The first term in relation (9.9) indicates the nominal appreciation of fixed assets, which equals

$$d\ FIXA = FIXA_t - FIXA_{t-1} - NEIN_t \qquad (9.10)$$

where $NEIN_t$ = net investment stated in year-end prices.

Relation (9.10) can be broken down into two components, inflation-compensation on the opening balance of assets and holding gains on fixed assets.

Holding Gains

Holding gains on fixed assets represent the increase in the assets' replacement value over and above the inflation-compensation on the opening balance of the assets. Specifically, holding gains are

$$A_{t-1}(1 + p_s) - A_{t-1}(1 + p)$$

where A_{t-1} = current replacement value of an asset at the beginning of the period,

p_s = specific price increase in year,

p = inflation rate in year t.

Given that the net investment is carried out evenly during the year, then the inflation compensation is

$$p \ FIXA_{t-1} + (p/2) \ NEIN \qquad (9.11)$$

where NEIj $=$ net investment stated in year's average prices.

And the formula for holding gains,[5] is

$$HG = FIXA_t - [(1 + p) \ FIXA_{t-1} + (1 + p/2) \ NEIN] \qquad (9.12)$$

As the level of the individual components of capital gains does not provide important information, capital gains can be calculated as the difference between total income—relation (9.1)—and operating income—relation (9.3).

NOTES

1. Financial Accounting Standards Board Statement No. 33 (1979) applies to large public enterprises in the United States. Historical costs of purchased inputs are adjusted in such a way to be stated in dollars valued according to the dates of usage. For details of the resulting bias, see Goldschmidt and Shashua (1984).

2. Such a procedure, called "gearing adjustment," is mandated in Great Britain by the Institute of Chartered Accountants in England and Wales (1980) and is used by N. V. Philips Industries in the Netherlands for reporting in hyper-inflationary countries (Enthoven, 1982, p. 25). For clarification, see Shashua, Goldschmidt and Hillman (1983).

3. About one half of the current assets in industry are financed by short-term loans. This is indicated by the current ratio—that is, the ratio of current assets to current liabilities. This ratio for 2,400 companies in all United States industries in 1975 was about two, with a distribution between one and four (Foster, 1978, p. 179).

4. The nominal investment plus the interest thereon is

$$INVS_t = INVS(s_{n,i}/n)$$

where $s_{n,i}$ $= \dfrac{(1 + i)^n - 1}{i}$

$\qquad\quad =$ future value of ordinary annuity,

$s_{n,i}/n \approx \sqrt{1 + r} \approx 1 + r/2$, for 12 months and moderate interest rates,

$\qquad i \ =$ periodic (monthly) interest rate,

$\qquad n \ =$ periods (12 months),

$\qquad r \ =$ annual interest rate.

5. It should be noted that holding gains on inventories are included in operating income (within the term d INVY), not in capital gains, because these gains are realized during the accounting year. Furthermore, usually these gains are not significant (when the FIFO—first in first out—method for inventory accounting is used), and the differentiation of these gains unnecessarily complicates the computations.

APPENDIX
TREATMENT OF EQUITY ADDITIONS AND
INCOME WITHDRAWALS

Total real income of a firm in a period can be determined by the change in equity (excluding new issues and withdrawals), between the opening and closing balance sheets, plus withdrawn income (dividends), measured in constant prices. The value of equity is equal to the value of assets at current replacement value less liabilities, stated at the price level of the balance sheet date. Thus, total real income of a firm, assuming no additions or withdrawals of equity and no paid-out dividends, is

$$R = (ASST_t - DEBT_t) - (1 + p)(ASST_{t-1} - DEBT_{t-1}) \qquad (9.13)$$

where ASST $\ =\ $ total assets at current replacement value,
     DEBT $\ =\ $ total liabilities,
  ASST $-$ DEBT $=$ equity,
     t, t-1 $\ =\ $ date of closing and opening balance sheets, respectively,
        p $\ =\ $ inflation rate between t and t-1.

Relation (9.13) provides the same income figure as relation (9.1).

If equity is added during the year, its value should be maintained equivalent to the value of the opening equity. Thus, the following variable should be subtracted from relation (9.13) or relation (9.1)

$$\sum_i (1 + p_i)(\text{Equity additions})_i \qquad (9.14)$$

where p_i = price level change between month i, when equity is added, and date t— the closing date of the balance sheet.

A firm's total income is usually composed of retained earnings and paid-out dividends. To arrive at a correct income figure, interim dividend payments should be compounded to the end of the year, using the firm's cost of capital, before adding these sums to the end-of-year figure for retained earnings. Under inflationary conditions, the same procedure should be carried out, using the nominal cost of capital. Thus, the following variable should be added to relation (9.13) or relation (9.1).

$$\sum_i (1 + r_i)\,\text{Dividend}_i \qquad (9.15)$$

where r_i = nominal cost of capital between month i, when dividend is paid, and date t.

The summation of relations (9.13) or (9.1) less relation (9.14) plus relation (9.15) provides total real income when equity is added and income is withdrawn during the year.

TEN

INCOME MEASUREMENT FOR THE UNITED STATES FARM SECTOR, 1950–1982

The model for income measurement under inflation developed in the preceding chapter is applied in this chapter to data for the United States farm sector. As shown in the preceding chapter, this model differs from the model used by the USDA Economic Research Service (ERS), especially as regards the estimation of operating income and capital gains. The main difference lies in the allocation of interest expense in calculating the two income components. The sum of these two income components, however, does not differ significantly from the ERS model.

The calculated income statements and balance sheets for the analyzed period are presented in both nominal and constant prices and trends.

10.1 PROCEDURES FOR CALCULATING INCOME OF THE UNITED STATES FARM SECTOR

Real income for the farm sector is computed and published annually by the ERS in "Economic Indicators of the Farm Sector—Income and Balance Sheet Statistics" (USDA, 1983, pp. 14, 15, 125, and 126). The model underlying the ERS procedure is, in principal, as follows:[1]

$$R = [SALES + d\ INVY_h - PURS - MANG - DEPR - INTR]$$
$$+ [d\ PHYA - p\ PHYA_{t-1} + p\ NETD_{t-1}] \qquad (10.1)$$

where $SALES + d\ INVY_h$ = gross receipts, excluding farm households,

$$d \ INVY_h \ = \ \text{net inventory change in year's average prices}$$
(USDA, 1983, pp. 6, 14, 65),

$PURS \ = \ $ materials, taxes, and labor (hired and operators' imputed cost),[2]

$DEPR \ = \ $ depreciation on current replacement costs of assets assumed to be recorded in year's average prices,

$INTR \ = \ $ interest on non-real estate and real estate debt,

$PHYA \ = \ FIXA + INVY = $ physical assets,

$FIXA \ = \ $ fixed assets, depreciated current replacement value,

$INVY \ = \ $ inventories at current replacement value,

$d \ PHYA \ = \ PHYA_t - PHYA_{t-1} - $ net investment,

Net investment $= \ $ gross investment minus depreciation,

$t, t-1 \ = \ $ date of closing and opening balance sheets, respectively,

$p \ = \ $ inflation rate between $t-1$ and t,

$NETD \ = \ $ debt minus financial assets,

$MANG \ = \ $ imputed cost of management.

Given that

$$d \ PHYA \ = \ d \ FIXA + d \ INVY$$
$$\text{and } EQTY \ = \ PHYA + \text{Financial assets} - \text{Debt}$$
$$= \ PHYA - NETD$$

Then, relation (10.1) is equal to relation (9.1) except for two terms which have been added in relation (10.1). The first term is MANG, the imputed cost of management; and the second is $d \ INVY_h$. The inclusion of the term $d \ INVY_h$ double-counts the change in the value of inventories—once in year's average prices in the first bracketed portion (as $d \ INVY_h$) and again in current prices in the second bracketed portion (as $d \ INVY$, which is included in $d \ PHYA$).[3]

The total real income as measured by relation (10.1) is composed of two components, each bracketed separately. The first is called "residual income to equity" and the second is called "real capital gains." Similarly, in the proposed model—relation (9.1)—total real income is broken down into two components: "operating income," as measured by relation (9.4) and "capital gains" as measured by relation (9.9). But there is a significant difference between the two models. Operating income in the proposed model differs from ERS's residual income to equity by the way the interest is charged, as shown below.[4]

To reduce the differences in the resulting figures of the first income component, relation (9.4) has been modified slightly to suit the formulation for the change in inventories and for including the imputed cost of management, as carried out by the ERS. Thus, the respective relations for the first income component are as follows:

$$\text{RITE} = \text{SALES} + \text{d INVY}_h - \text{PURS} - \text{MANG}$$
$$- \text{DEPR} - \text{INTR} \qquad (10.2)$$
$$\text{OI}_M = \text{SALES} + \text{d INVY}_h - \text{PURS} - \text{MANG}$$
$$- \text{DEPR} - \text{I}_C - \text{I}_F \qquad (10.3)$$

where RITE = residual income to equity,

OI_M = operating income—based on relation (9.4)—after management expense,

I_C = imputed interest on working capital (current assets), as shown below,

I_F = imputed interest on loans financing fixed assets, as shown below.

Interest on working capital, I_C, is determined as an imputed cost, based on the actual average interest rate on non-real estate debt, as explained and carried out in section 4.2.

Interest on loans financing fixed assets is determined by applying a normative inflation-free interest to the balance of debt at the beginning of the year. The normative interest rate is set at 3 percent— which is an estimate of the long-run average inflation-free interest rate actually paid by the farm sector.[5] The debt financing fixed assets is the difference between total debt and current assets, at the beginning of the year, and this difference is then inflated to the end of the year; that is,

$$\text{I}_F = 0.03(1 + p)\,(\text{debt} - \text{current assets}) \qquad (10.4)$$

The modification of relation (9.4) into relation (10.3) implies a corresponding modification of relation (9.9) for measuring capital gains, to be stated as follows:

$$\text{CG} = \text{d FIXA} + \text{d INVY} - \text{p EQTY}$$
$$- (\text{INTR} - \text{I}_C - \text{I}_F) - \text{d INVY}_h \qquad (10.5)$$

where CG = capital gains,

d FIXA = nominal appreciation of fixed assets, at current replacement values, less net investment (gross investment less depreciation), d INVY = nominal change in current replacement values of inventories,

p EQTY = equity maintenance = inflation rate applied to opening balance of equity at current value.

In other words, to avoid double counting the change in value of inventories, the term d $INVY_h$ is deducted from capital gains.

The main factor affecting capital gains in the farm sector is holding gains on land—representing the increase in land value over and above the increase in value implied by the rise in the general price level. Therefore this variable is measured and reported separately in analyzing income statements in section 10.4.

10.2 APPLICATION OF THE PROCEDURES TO FINANCIAL STATEMENTS FOR 1982

The procedures outlined in the preceding section are applied in this section to calculate the income of the United States farm sector for 1982, based on balance sheets for January 1982 and January 1983.

To calculate the two categories of imputed interest and to measure holding gains on land, we use a classification of assets in the balance sheets of the farm sector that differs slightly from that used by the ERS.

Assets in the balance sheets of the United States farm sector are grouped here into two categories, current and fixed. Assets that are realized during the accounting year are considered current, whereas those that provide services over several accounting years are considered fixed. Thus, short-term financial assets, inventories of crops, and livestock-in-process, are considered current assets; livestock that are kept for several years, investment in cooperatives, machinery, structures, and land are considered fixed assets.

In determining the level of working capital in section 4.1, the data on the aggregate value of livestock is differentiated into livestock-in-process (current assets), including feeders, calves, lambs, and so on, and the rest of the livestock (fixed assets) such as beef cows, milking cows, ewes, and so on. One quarter of the total stock of animals is considered livestock-in-process.

Balance sheets for the United States farm sector for January 1982 and January 1983 are presented in table 10.1. The figures in table 10.1 are presented in nominal prices. Thus, before comparing opening and closing figures, these must be stated in constant prices, as shown in the next section.

Table 10.1   Balance Sheets, U.S. Farm Sector, 1982, Replacement Values, Excluding Farm Households (billion dollars)

	January 1982		January 1983	
Assets				
Current assets:				
Deposits and currency	7.5		7.8	
Crops stored	36.3		42.1	
Livestock in process[a]	13.4		13.2	
Total current assets		57.2		63.1
Fixed assets:[b]				
Livestock	40.2		39.7	
Investment in cooperatives	24.6		26.8	
Equipment	103.0		105.8	
Structures	45.3		42.2	
Land	709.3		670.0	
Total fixed assets		922.4		884.5
Total assets		979.6		947.6
Liabilities and equity				
Short-term:				
Non-real estate debt	91.5		102.0	
Real estate debt	97.0		100.8	
Total debt		188.5		202.8
Equity		791.2		744.9
Total liabilities and equity		979.7		947.7

[a]One quarter of the total livestock is assumed to be of short-term nature (feeders, calves, and so on).
[b]Including investments.
Source: USDA (1983) pp. 105, 106, 110.

The income statement for the United States farm sector for 1982, as computed by relations (10.3) and (10.5), is presented in table 10.2 alongside the ERS's income statement (USDA, 1983, pp. 125, 126). The two income statements in table 10.2 differ in interest expenses, which affect residual income to equity (but not total income), and in capital gains, which affect total income. Estimates of the income components under the USDA-ERS and the proposed models, for the period 1950–1982, are presented in appendix table 10.G.

For calculating the two types of imputed interest charges, consider the main items of the farm sector's balance sheet for January 1982, as depicted in figure 10.1. The scheme in figure 10.1 shows that in 1982 equity is attributed to finance the land and a portion of the other fixed assets. Debt is attributed to finance current assets and

Table 10.2   Income Statement, U.S. Farm Sector, 1982 (billion dollars)

	USDA-ERS[a]		Proposed Model	
Gross receipts[b]		149.6		149.6
Expenses:				
Materials and taxes		78.0		78.0
Labor, hired	10.8		10.8	
Labor, operators' imputed cost	4.5		4.5	
		15.3		15.3
Depreciation[c]		19.8		19.8
Interest,[d] short-term loans	11.3		5.9	
Interest, long-term loans	9.6		4.1	
		20.9		10.0
Total expenses		134.0		123.1
Operating income, before management				26.5
Management, imputed cost		6.0		6.0
Residual income to equity		9.6		
Operating income after management				20.5
Capital Gains:				
Nominal change in assets value[e]				(34.4)
Equity maintenance[f]				(28.0)
Difference in interest[h]				(10.9)
Change in inventories[i]				(6.5)
Capital gains		(60.9)[g]		(79.8)
Total income, after management		(51.3)		(59.3)
Total income, before management		(45.3)		(53.3)

[a]*Source:* USDA (1983), pp. 14, 15, 125, 126. Excluding farm households.
[b]Including 6.5 net change in inventories.
[c]Based on replacement value.
[d]ERS: interest on non-real estate and real estate debt, respectively. Proposed model: imputed interest on working capital and on loans financing fixed assets, respectively.
[e]d FIXA + d INVY, from relation (10.5); figures are taken from USDA (1983), p. 126.
[f]Inflation compensation on equity at beginning of year; 791.2 × 3.5448%.
[g]Stated at beginning-of-year prices.
[h]Difference between actual expenses (20.9) and imputed charges (10.0).
[i]To eliminate the double count.

$131.3 billion of the fixed assets. Interest on the debt that finances current assets (interest on working capital) is estimated in section 4.3 to be $5.9 billion. This sum, which is in nominal terms, is charged in conjunction with the expenses that are recorded as historical costs. The imputed interest on debt that finances fixed assets for 1982 is computed by relation (10.4) as follows:

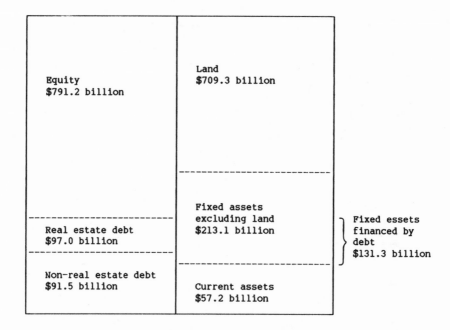

Fig. 10.1 Scheme of a balance sheet, U.S. farm sector, January 1982

$$I_F = 0.03(1 + 0.035448)(188.5 - 57.2) = \$4.1 \text{ billion}$$

This sum, which is in real inflation-free terms, is charged in conjunction with the depreciation on revalued assets. The difference between actual interest expenses and imputed interest charges—relation (9.8)—is

$$INTR - I_C - I_F = 20.9 - 5.9 - 4.1 = \$10.9 \text{ billion}$$

This balance represents the actual premium, or inflation-compensation, on the loans financing fixed assets which is embodied in the interest rate; therefore it is considered capital gains—relation (10.5). This sum also provides the difference between the ERS's residual income to equity and the corresponding figure of the proposed model—operating income after management—as shown in table 10.2.

When current assets are financed partially by equity, as happened in the United States farm sector until 1957, imputed real interest at 3 percent is credited against the imputed nominal interest charge on working capital. This procedure is carried out automatically by the three relations (10.3)–(10.5).[6] In other words, when the level of total debt exceeds the level of current assets, interest at 3 percent is charged as a cost for the service of loans financing fixed assets; when the opposite holds, interest at 3 percent is credited against the costs for the equity financing current assets. The results of applying this procedure can be seen in appendix table 10.E.

Imputed charge for management is debited while computing residual income to equity, as shown in table 10.2, but this charge is excluded from operating income.

Capital gains can be computed by either applying relation (10.5), as carried out in table 10.2, or by subtracting operating income from total income, as carried out in table 10.5. Capital gains, as computed by relation (10.5) and presented in table 10.2, amounted in 1982 to −$79.8 billion. The sources of this loss are (1) decline in land value, in real terms (holding gains on land) of −$64.4 billion; (2) inflation-compensation on loans financing fixed assets of −$10.9 billion; (3) decline in real value of inventories of −$6.5 billion; and (4) real gain of $2 billion on other balance sheet items. The holding loss on land, for 1982, is calculated by relation (9.12) as follows:

$$670.0 - (1 + 0.035448)709.3 = -\$64.4 \text{ billion}$$

Capital gains or losses indicate changes in wealth that accrue to a firm mainly by exogeneous factors, not controllable by the firm. Moreover, these figures are meaningful only in the case that a firm or part of its land is sold. But for a sector, the figures on capital gains do not convey important information that can be used in performance evaluation.

10.3 PRESENTATION OF BALANCE SHEETS FOR 1950–1982

To compare and analyze financial statements for a series of years, the corresponding figures should be stated either in constant prices— that is, inflated by the Consumer Price Index to the latest date in the series, or in common size form—that is, the components of the statements are presented as percentages of the totals. The first type of presentation makes it possible to check the trends in the individual items, while the second enables the analyst to check the composition of the statements.

The main balance sheet components for the United States farm sector for some selected years are presented in the top of table 10.3.. The individual items, in both nominal and constant prices, are presented in appendix tables 10.B and 10.D. As can be seen, the value reflected in the balance sheet, in January 1983 prices, more

Table 10.3 Balance Sheets of the U.S. Farm Sector, Main Items, Selected Years

	Jan. 1950	Jan. 1960	Jan. 1970	Jan. 1980	Jan. 1983	Increase 1983–1950	Growth (1983/1950)
A. Values in billion dollars in January 1983 prices							
Current assets	73.9	58.8	59.7	70.3	63.1	−10.8	0.85
Fixed assets, excl. land	138.3	166.8	183.6	251.5	214.5	76.2	1.55
Land	226.6	348.3	454.3	816.2	670.0	443.4	2.96
Total[a]	438.8	573.9	697.6	1138.0	947.6	508.8	2.15
Debt	46.4	74.8	126.1	193.9	202.8	156.4	4.37
Equity	392.0	499.8	571.3	944.2	744.9	352.9	1.90
Total[a]	438.4	574.6	697.4	1138.1	947.7	509.3	
B. Composition in percentages							
Current assets	16.8	10.2	8.6	6.2	6.7		
Fixed assets excl. land	31.5	29.1	26.3	22.1	22.6		
Land	51.7	60.7	65.1	71.7	70.7		
Total	100.0	100.0	100.0	100.0	100.0		

[a]Imbalances result from rounding nominal data.
Source: Appendix table 10.C.

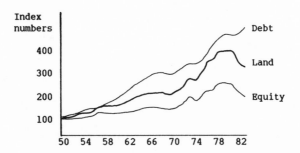

Fig. 10.2 Growth in main items of the balance
sheet, in constant prices, U.S. farm sector

than doubled in the analyzed period from about $440 billion in
January 1950 to about $950 billion in January 1983, with a peak of
$1,140 billion in January 1980. The main contributors to this trend
were land value, which tripled, in constant prices, during the period,
and machinery, which doubled in value. On the other hand, the
volume of debt increased, in constant prices, more than four-fold
during the period, while the value of equity doubled.

The growth trend of the main balance sheet items over the analyzed
period, stated as index numbers, is presented in figure 10.2. The
graphs indicate the trend, in constant prices, relative to January 1950
values, which are stated as 100.

The relative level of the three main types of assets, for some
selected years, is presented in section B of table 10.3. The share of
land increased from about 50 percent of the balance sheet in 1950
to about 70 percent in the early 1980s. As a result, the share of the
other assets decreased.

The level of the individual items composing current assets and
debt is presented in earlier chapters—in tables 4.1 and 8.1, respectively.
The level of the individual items composing fixed assets excluding
land is presented in table 10.4.

The value of fixed assets excluding land, in constant prices, increased
during the analyzed period by about 50 percent, but the rate of
growth of the individual items differed considerably. The value of
both livestock and structures, in constant prices, did not change in
the analyzed period, whereas the value of the other items increased
considerably—the value of investment in cooperatives tripled, and
the value of machinery more than doubled.

The figures in section B of table 10.4 show that the share for
machinery and structures was equal in 1950. Stagnation in the value

Table 10.4   Fixed Assets Excluding Land and Households, U.S. Farm Sector, Selected Years

	Jan. 1950	Jan. 1960	Jan. 1970	Jan. 1980	Jan. 1983	Increase 1983– 1950	Growth (1983/ 1950)
A. Values in billion dollars in January 1983 prices							
Livestock	40.1	37.9	45.4	57.7	39.7	−0.4	0.99
Investment in cooperatives	8.7	14.0	18.6	26.0	26.8	18.1	3.08
Machinery	44.8	64.0	73.2	113.7	105.8	61.0	2.34
Structures	44.7	50.8	46.4	54.1	42.2	−2.5	0.94
Total[a]	138.3	166.7	183.6	251.5	214.5	76.2	1.55
B. Composition in percentages							
Livestock	29.0	22.7	24.7	22.9	18.5		
Investment in cooperatives	6.3	8.4	10.1	10.3	12.5		
Machinery	32.4	38.4	39.9	45.2	49.3		
Structures	32.3	30.5	25.3	21.5	19.7		
Total	100.0	100.0	100.0	100.0	100.0		

Source: Appendix table 10.D.

of structures and the significant growth in the value of machinery changed the relative share of these items. The share of investment in cooperatives increased from a negligible level of 6 percent in 1950 to over 12 percent in 1983, while the share of livestock declined.

The increase in the value of the fixed assets excluding land of $76.2 billion (from $138.3 billion in 1950 to $214.5 billion in 1983— table 10.4) resulted mainly from capital formation ($71 billion, as shown in section 11.4). This fact implies that holding gains on these assets were relatively small.

The main factor contributing to growth of the United States farm sector was land, the value of which, in constant prices, tripled during the 33-year period. In other words, while the volume of land was more or less stable, its value increased, in real terms, by about 3.44 percent per annum over the whole period. The annual increase during the period January 1950 to January 1980 was 4.52 percent per annum, whereas during the period January 1980 to January 1983, a decline of 6.49 percent per annum was experienced.

The highest rate of appreciation in land value was during the 1970s—a 6.2 percent growth per annum, in constant prices, between 1971 and 1980. This trend can be partially attributed to inflation.

Because land provides an excellent tax shelter during inflation (chapter 7), the demand for land and its price increase.

The increase in land value of about $440 billion between 1950 and 1983 (section A of table 10.3), resulting from holding gains, should have raised the value of equity at least by this amount. However, the value of equity rose, during this period, by only $350 billion (table 10.3). This phenomenon suggests that equity was withdrawn from the sector and debt substituted for it, as will be shown in section 11.5.

10.4 PRESENTATION OF INCOME STATEMENTS FOR 1950–1982

Income figures for a series of years can be compared by presenting the data in constant prices, in the same way as balance sheet items where both are stated in year-end prices (using the Consumer Price Index). Stating the other items of the income statement in constant prices, on the other hand, requires using a year's average specific price index for each item. These calculations for gross receipts, total costs, and labor costs are carried out and presented in appendix table 11.D. Instead of presenting income statements in common size form, some ratios of income and inputs to gross receipts are calculated and presented in the next chapter.

The individual income components for the United States farm sector, in constant prices, for the analyzed period 1950–1982 are presented in table 10.5. The corresponding figures in nominal prices and the main expense items appear in appendix tables 10.E and 10.F. The figures in table 10.5 show that operating income before deducting management expense, in constant prices, is relatively constant, averaging about $29 billion per year, in January 1983 prices. The highest level was in 1973 ($71 billion), and the lowest in 1955 and 1959 (about $15 billion). Capital gains, on the other hand, fluctuated from a loss of over $100 billion in 1981 to a gain of close to $100 billion in 1976, in January 1983 prices. These fluctuations are shown in figure 10.3.

To illustrate the relative share of the individual income components, consider the sums of these components for the 33-year period, as presented in the foot of table 10.5. Deducting the total of imputed cost of management ($177 billion) from the total operating income, leaves $765 billion as residual income to equity. This figure comprises about 60 percent of the total income after management expense (1427

Table 10.5   Income Components, U.S. Farm Sector, 1950–1982 (billion dollars in January 1983 prices)

Year	Operating Income, Before Management	Capital Gains	Total Income Before Management	Management, Imputed Cost	Holding Gains on Land
1950	26.61	18.24	44.85	4.61	17.48
1951	30.29	10.74	41.04	5.16	14.83
1952	25.57	−17.79	7.78	5.12	3.50
1953	18.31	−8.34	9.97	4.71	−5.46
1954	18.32	−10.09	8.23	4.74	13.96
1955	15.34	18.87	34.21	4.37	16.06
1956	15.73	19.33	35.06	4.23	15.32
1957	16.31	12.61	28.92	4.43	8.17
1958	24.02	32.03	56.05	4.71	22.65
1959	15.20	4.79	19.99	4.32	15.10
1960	19.31	−1.96	17.35	4.58	0.76
1961	22.42	20.10	42.52	4.87	15.54
1962	24.06	14.76	38.82	4.81	12.51
1963	23.66	11.16	34.82	5.05	17.55
1964	20.75	22.64	43.38	4.68	20.44
1965	30.42	31.72	62.14	5.21	23.40
1966	33.02	19.47	52.49	5.33	11.25
1967	25.65	9.60	35.25	5.15	12.22
1968	24.46	7.15	31.61	5.20	3.20
1969	28.15	−6.24	21.91	5.16	−10.85
1970	27.58	−6.12	21.47	5.15	−5.09
1971	27.44	25.42	52.85	5.22	19.79
1972	39.46	61.76	101.22	5.72	37.91
1973	71.44	87.41	158.86	7.53	64.35
1974	48.63	0.24	48.87	6.74	−7.06
1975	42.60	59.08	101.68	6.66	53.67
1976	31.43	99.82	131.25	6.17	83.33
1977	28.44	37.22	65.67	6.09	36.80
1978	39.17	90.96	130.12	6.56	63.12
1979	42.10	17.25	59.36	6.76	15.10
1980	26.28	−12.01	14.27	6.05	−14.41
1981	33.93	−104.75	−70.82	6.42	−67.35
1982	26.53	−80.42	−53.35	6.00	−64.44
Total	942.63	484.68	1427.86	177.49	443.36
Average	28.56	14.69	43.27	5.38	13.44

− 177 = 1250); the rest is made up of capital gains, of which more than 90 percent are holding gains on land ($443 billion out of $485 billion). The actual allocation of annual income to equity (as retained earnings) or to other uses outside the farm sector (withdrawal of income) is analyzed in section 11.5.

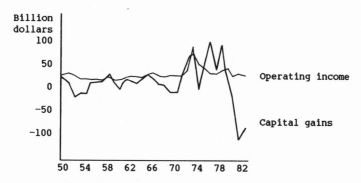

Fig. 10.3   Income components, January 1983 prices,
U.S. farm sector (table 10.5)

NOTES

1. The prevailing procedure for measuring real income for the United States farm sector is explained in USDA (1983) pp. 11-12, and in Hottel and Evans (1980). For an earlier model see Melichar (1979).

2. Imputed cost of operators' labor is charged separately (USDA, 1983, p. 125).

3. There is another difference, resulting from a computational error: The second bracketed portion in relation (10.1) is discounted to the beginning of the year (USDA, 1983, p. 126 and personal communication).

4. It should be noted that Hill (1984) also charges imputed interest in measuring farm income in England. He uses real interest throughout, because the cost of goods sold are revalued, not the depreciation alone.

5. During the period 1951-1972, when the inflation rate was low, the average inflation-free rate was 2.95 percent (appendix table 8.A).

6. Consider the data for 1950, where the level of current assets is higher than the level of total debt (appendix table 10.A). Interest on operating capital is estimated to be $0.68 billion (section 4.3), whereas total interest expenses are $0.56 billion. This imputed nominal interest charge should be accompanied by imputed credit to the equity, as is automatically carried out by relations (10.3)–(10.5). Applying relation (10.4),

$$I_F = 0.03(1 + 0.079433)(11.2 - 17.8) = -\$0.21 \text{ billion,}$$

the negative sum means that the equity, which finances the current asset, earns $0.21 billion imputed interest charges, based on 3 percent inflation-free interest. This figure is independent of the maintenance of equity purchasing power.

APPENDIX

Appendix Table 10.A Balance Sheets of the U.S. Farm Sector, January 1950–January 1983 (billion dollars in nominal prices)

Year	Current Assets	Fixed Assets Excluding Land	Land	Total Assets	Non-Real Estate Debt	Real Estate Debt	Total Debt	Equity	Total Liabilities
1950	17.83	33.38	54.70	105.90	6.50	4.70	11.20	94.60	105.80
1951	19.18	39.73	63.60	122.50	6.50	5.20	11.70	110.80	122.50
1952	20.98	44.73	70.30	136.00	7.40	5.70	13.10	122.90	136.00
1953	19.80	42.20	71.70	133.70	8.30	6.20	14.50	119.30	133.80
1954	19.03	40.38	71.00	130.40	8.70	6.60	15.30	115.10	130.40
1955	19.30	40.30	74.30	133.90	8.90	7.10	16.00	118.10	134.10
1956	17.85	40.95	78.90	137.70	9.20	7.80	17.00	120.80	137.80
1957	17.75	42.85	85.70	146.30	8.90	8.50	17.40	128.90	146.30
1958	17.58	45.63	91.10	154.30	9.40	9.00	18.40	136.00	154.40
1959	20.63	50.48	99.00	170.10	11.80	9.70	21.50	148.70	170.20
1960	17.70	50.20	104.80	172.70	11.90	10.60	22.50	150.40	172.90
1961	17.70	50.30	106.70	174.70	12.50	11.30	23.80	150.90	174.70
1962	18.70	51.60	112.20	182.50	13.60	12.30	25.90	156.70	182.60
1963	19.53	53.18	117.60	190.30	15.30	13.40	28.70	161.60	190.30
1964	19.48	53.33	125.10	197.90	16.50	14.90	31.40	166.50	197.90
1965	18.63	53.88	133.00	205.50	16.90	16.80	33.70	171.80	205.50

Year									
1966	20.10	58.30	143.20	221.60	18.30	18.90	37.20	184.30	221.50
1967	20.75	61.85	151.80	234.40	19.70	20.70	40.40	194.00	234.40
1968	20.40	64.90	161.30	246.60	21.00	22.60	43.60	203.00	246.60
1969	21.95	67.95	169.90	259.80	21.80	24.70	46.50	213.40	259.90
1970	23.18	71.23	176.20	270.60	22.70	26.20	48.90	221.60	270.50
1971	23.13	73.68	183.30	280.10	23.10	27.40	50.50	229.70	280.20
1972	25.33	79.98	197.80	303.10	26.20	29.10	55.30	247.70	303.00
1973	30.03	89.98	221.60	341.60	28.50	31.70	60.20	281.20	341.40
1974	39.70	106.10	273.20	419.00	32.30	35.80	68.10	350.80	418.90
1975	36.23	104.28	301.50	442.00	35.30	40.50	75.80	366.30	442.10
1976	35.65	121.95	352.60	510.20	40.00	45.10	85.10	425.10	510.20
1977	36.25	133.45	420.80	590.50	46.50	50.30	96.80	493.80	590.60
1978	39.88	144.53	472.70	657.00	56.90	57.80	114.70	542.30	657.00
1979	48.03	174.98	561.40	784.40	66.30	65.40	131.70	652.70	784.40
1980	56.15	200.85	651.90	908.90	76.50	78.40	154.90	754.10	909.00
1981	58.50	212.10	715.60	986.20	82.30	87.70	170.00	816.10	986.10
1982	57.20	213.10	709.30	979.60	91.50	97.00	188.50	791.20	979.70
1983	63.13	214.48	670.00	947.60	102.00	100.80	202.80	744.90	947.70

Source: USDA (1983). Replacement values; excluding farm households.

Appendix Table 10.B   Assets, the U.S. Farm Sector, January 1950–January 1983 (billion dollars in nominal prices)

Year	Financial Assets	Crops Stored	Livestock in Process	Livestock	Investments in Cooperatives	Machinery	Structures	Land	Total
1950	7.00	7.60	3.23	9.68	2.10	10.80	10.80	54.70	105.90
1951	7.00	7.90	4.28	12.83	2.30	12.30	12.30	63.60	122.50
1952	7.30	8.80	4.88	14.63	2.50	14.30	13.30	70.30	136.00
1953	7.10	9.00	3.70	11.10	2.70	15.00	13.40	71.70	133.70
1954	7.00	9.10	2.93	8.78	2.90	15.60	13.10	71.00	130.40
1955	6.90	9.60	2.80	8.40	3.00	15.70	13.20	74.30	133.90
1956	6.90	8.30	2.65	7.95	3.20	16.30	13.50	78.90	137.70
1957	6.70	8.30	2.75	8.25	3.50	16.90	14.20	85.70	146.30
1958	6.50	7.60	3.48	10.43	3.70	17.00	14.50	91.10	154.30
1959	6.90	9.30	4.43	13.28	3.90	18.10	15.20	99.00	170.10
1960	6.20	7.70	3.80	11.40	4.20	19.30	15.30	104.80	172.70
1961	5.80	8.00	3.90	11.70	4.50	19.00	15.10	106.70	174.70
1962	5.80	8.80	4.10	12.30	4.80	19.20	15.30	112.20	182.50
1963	5.90	9.30	4.33	12.98	5.00	19.80	15.40	117.60	190.30
1964	5.70	9.80	3.98	11.93	5.40	20.20	15.80	125.10	197.90
1965	5.80	9.20	3.63	10.88	5.60	21.10	16.30	133.00	205.50
1966	6.00	9.70	4.40	13.20	5.90	22.20	17.00	143.20	221.60

Year									
1967	6.00	10.00	4.75	14.25	6.20	23.80	17.60	151.80	234.40
1968	6.10	9.60	4.70	14.10	6.50	26.10	18.20	161.30	246.60
1969	6.30	10.60	5.05	15.15	6.80	27.50	18.50	169.90	259.80
1970	6.40	10.90	5.88	17.63	7.20	28.40	18.00	176.20	270.60
1971	6.50	10.70	5.93	17.78	8.00	30.00	17.90	183.30	280.10
1972	6.70	11.80	6.83	20.48	8.80	32.10	18.60	197.80	303.10
1973	7.00	14.50	8.53	25.58	9.80	34.40	20.20	221.60	341.60
1974	7.10	22.00	10.60	31.80	10.90	39.50	23.90	273.20	419.00
1975	6.80	23.30	6.13	18.38	11.40	49.10	25.40	301.50	442.00
1976	7.00	21.30	7.35	22.05	13.40	58.10	28.40	352.60	510.20
1977	6.90	22.10	7.25	21.75	14.90	64.10	32.70	420.80	590.50
1978	7.10	24.80	7.98	23.93	15.40	70.30	34.90	472.70	657.10
1979	7.20	28.00	12.83	38.48	18.30	78.70	39.50	561.40	784.40
1980	7.30	33.50	15.35	46.05	20.80	90.80	43.20	651.90	908.90
1981	7.40	35.90	15.20	45.60	22.80	96.80	46.90	715.60	986.20
1982	7.50	36.30	13.40	40.20	24.60	103.00	45.30	709.30	979.60
1983	7.80	42.10	13.23	39.68	26.80	105.80	42.20	670.00	947.60

Source: USDA (1983). Replacement values; excluding farm households.

Appendix Table 10.C   Balance Sheets of the U.S. Farm Sector, January 1950–January 1983 (billion dollars in January 1983 prices)

Year	Current Assets	Fixed Assets Excluding Land	Land	Total Assets	Non-Real Estate Debt	Real Estate Debt	Total Debt	Equity	Total Liabilities
1950	73.85	138.28	226.64	438.77	26.93	19.47	46.40	391.95	438.36
1951	73.60	152.48	244.12	470.20	24.95	19.96	44.91	425.29	470.20
1952	77.26	164.74	258.95	500.95	27.26	21.00	48.25	452.70	500.95
1953	72.48	154.47	262.45	489.40	30.38	22.69	53.08	436.69	489.76
1954	68.86	146.14	256.99	471.99	31.49	23.89	55.38	416.61	471.99
1955	70.38	146.96	270.95	488.29	32.46	25.89	58.35	430.67	489.02
1956	64.93	148.96	287.01	500.90	33.47	28.37	61.84	439.42	501.26
1957	62.62	151.17	302.33	516.11	31.40	29.99	61.38	454.73	516.11
1958	59.90	155.51	310.51	525.92	32.04	30.68	62.71	463.54	526.26
1959	69.41	169.86	333.16	572.42	39.71	32.64	72.35	500.41	572.76
1960	58.82	166.82	348.26	573.90	39.54	35.22	74.77	499.79	574.56
1961	57.90	164.53	349.02	571.44	40.89	36.96	77.85	493.59	571.44
1962	60.76	167.66	364.56	592.97	44.19	39.96	84.15	509.14	593.30
1963	62.60	170.50	377.07	610.17	49.06	42.97	92.02	518.15	610.17
1964	61.43	168.21	394.62	624.26	52.05	47.00	99.05	525.21	624.26
1965	58.12	168.13	415.06	641.31	52.74	52.43	105.17	536.14	641.31
1966	61.54	178.51	438.46	678.50	56.03	57.87	113.90	564.30	678.20

Year									
1967	61.47	183.23	449.70	694.40	58.36	61.32	119.68	574.72	694.40
1968	58.42	185.86	461.92	706.19	60.14	64.72	124.86	581.34	706.19
1969	60.09	186.02	465.12	711.22	59.68	67.62	127.30	584.20	711.50
1970	59.75	183.63	454.26	697.64	58.52	67.55	126.07	571.31	697.38
1971	56.67	180.54	449.18	686.39	56.61	67.14	123.75	562.88	686.63
1972	60.04	189.62	468.97	718.63	62.12	68.99	131.11	587.28	718.40
1973	68.68	205.81	506.89	781.37	65.19	72.51	137.70	643.21	780.92
1974	83.01	221.85	571.24	876.09	67.54	74.85	142.39	733.49	875.88
1975	67.79	195.12	564.18	827.09	66.05	75.79	141.84	685.43	827.27
1976	62.47	213.69	617.84	894.00	70.09	79.03	149.12	744.88	894.00
1977	60.40	222.37	701.17	983.94	77.48	83.81	161.30	822.81	984.11
1978	62.25	225.63	737.98	1025.86	88.83	90.24	179.07	846.64	1025.71
1979	68.53	249.68	801.10	1119.31	94.61	93.32	187.93	931.38	1119.31
1980	70.30	251.47	816.20	1137.98	95.78	98.16	193.94	944.16	1138.10
1981	65.55	237.65	801.79	1104.98	92.21	98.26	190.48	914.40	1104.87
1982	59.23	220.65	734.44	1014.33	94.74	100.44	195.18	819.25	1014.43
1983	63.13	214.48	670.00	947.60	102.00	100.80	202.80	744.90	947.70

Source: Appendix table 10.A.

Appendix Table 10.D Assets, U.S. Farm Sector, January 1950–January 1983 (billion dollars in January 1983 prices)

Year	Financial Assets	Crops Stored	Livestock in Process	Livestock	Investments in Cooperatives	Machinery	Structures	Land	Total
1950	29.00	31.49	13.36	40.09	8.70	44.75	44.75	226.64	438.77
1951	26.87	30.32	16.41	49.23	8.83	47.21	47.21	244.12	470.20
1952	26.89	32.41	17.96	53.87	9.21	52.67	48.99	258.95	500.95
1953	25.99	32.94	13.54	40.63	9.88	54.91	49.05	262.45	489.40
1954	25.34	32.94	10.59	31.76	10.50	56.47	47.42	256.99	471.99
1955	25.16	35.01	10.21	30.63	10.94	57.25	48.14	270.95	488.29
1956	25.10	30.19	9.64	28.92	11.64	59.29	49.11	287.01	500.90
1957	23.64	29.28	9.70	29.10	12.35	59.62	50.09	302.33	516.11
1958	22.15	25.90	11.84	35.53	12.61	57.94	49.42	310.51	525.92
1959	23.22	31.30	14.89	44.67	13.12	60.91	51.15	333.16	572.42
1960	20.60	25.59	12.63	37.88	13.96	64.14	50.84	348.26	573.90
1961	18.97	26.17	12.76	38.27	14.72	62.15	49.39	349.02	571.44
1962	18.85	28.59	13.32	39.96	15.60	62.38	49.71	364.56	592.97
1963	18.92	29.82	13.87	41.60	16.03	63.49	49.38	377.07	610.17
1964	17.98	30.91	12.54	37.62	17.03	63.72	49.84	394.62	624.26
1965	18.10	28.71	11.31	33.94	17.48	65.85	50.87	415.06	641.31
1966	18.37	29.70	13.47	40.42	18.06	67.97	52.05	438.46	678.50
1967	17.77	29.62	14.07	42.22	18.37	70.51	52.14	449.70	694.40

1968	17.47	27.49	13.46	40.38	18.61	74.74	52.12	461.92	706.19
1969	17.25	29.02	13.82	41.47	18.62	75.28	50.65	465.12	711.22
1970	16.50	28.10	15.15	45.44	18.56	73.22	46.41	454.26	697.64
1971	15.93	26.22	14.52	43.56	19.60	73.52	43.86	449.18	686.39
1972	15.89	27.98	16.18	48.55	20.86	76.11	44.10	468.97	718.63
1973	16.01	33.17	19.50	58.50	22.42	78.69	46.21	506.89	781.37
1974	14.85	46.00	22.16	66.49	22.79	82.59	49.97	571.24	876.09
1975	12.72	43.60	11.46	34.38	21.33	91.88	47.53	564.18	827.09
1976	12.27	37.32	12.88	38.64	23.48	101.81	49.76	617.84	894.00
1977	11.50	36.82	12.08	36.24	24.83	106.81	54.49	701.17	983.94
1978	11.08	38.72	12.45	37.35	24.04	109.75	54.49	737.98	1025.86
1979	10.27	39.96	18.30	54.90	26.11	112.30	56.37	801.10	1119.31
1980	9.14	41.94	19.22	57.66	26.04	113.68	54.09	816.20	1137.98
1981	8.29	40.22	17.03	51.09	25.55	108.46	52.55	801.79	1104.98
1982	7.77	37.59	13.88	41.63	25.47	106.65	46.91	734.44	1014.33
1983	7.80	42.10	13.23	39.68	26.80	105.80	42.20	670.00	947.60

Source: Appendix table 10.B.

Table 10.E Income Statements, U.S. Farm Sector, 1950–1982 (billion dollars in nominal prices)

Year	Gross Farm Receipts[a]	Expenses Excluding Management	Operating Income	Capital Gains	Total Income	Management, Imputed Cost[a]	Holding Gains on Land
1950	31.90	24.97	6.93	4.75	11.69	1.20	4.56
1951	37.00	28.78	8.22	2.92	11.14	1.40	4.03
1952	36.30	29.31	6.99	−4.86	2.13	1.40	0.96
1953	32.90	27.84	5.06	−2.30	2.75	1.30	−1.51
1954	32.70	27.68	5.02	−2.77	2.26	1.30	3.83
1955	32.00	27.78	4.22	5.19	9.41	1.20	4.41
1956	32.50	28.04	4.46	5.48	9.94	1.20	4.34
1957	33.20	28.42	4.78	3.70	8.49	1.30	2.40
1958	37.30	30.16	7.14	9.52	16.65	1.40	6.73
1959	36.10	31.53	4.57	1.44	6.02	1.30	4.55
1960	37.10	31.20	5.90	−0.60	5.30	1.40	0.23
1961	38.60	31.70	6.90	6.19	13.09	1.50	4.78
1962	40.40	32.90	7.50	4.60	12.11	1.50	3.90
1963	41.30	33.80	7.50	3.54	11.04	1.60	5.56
1964	40.10	33.45	6.65	7.25	13.90	1.50	6.55
1965	44.30	34.36	9.94	10.36	20.30	1.70	7.64

1966	48.10	36.95	11.15	6.57	17.72	1.80	3.80
1967	48.00	39.04	8.96	3.35	12.31	1.80	4.27
1968	49.20	40.27	8.93	2.61	11.55	1.90	1.17
1969	53.60	42.68	10.92	-2.42	8.50	2.00	-4.21
1970	55.80	44.54	11.26	-2.50	8.76	2.10	-2.08
1971	58.90	47.33	11.57	10.72	22.29	2.20	8.35
1972	67.70	50.45	17.25	27.00	44.25	2.50	16.58
1973	95.10	60.93	34.17	41.81	75.98	3.60	30.78
1974	93.60	67.61	25.99	0.13	26.12	3.60	-3.77
1975	95.40	71.09	24.31	33.72	58.03	3.80	30.63
1976	96.90	78.04	18.86	59.91	78.77	3.70	50.01
1977	101.60	83.38	18.22	23.84	42.06	3.90	23.57
1978	119.30	91.85	27.45	63.74	91.19	4.60	44.23
1979	141.20	107.57	33.63	13.78	47.41	5.40	12.06
1980	139.40	115.94	23.46	-10.72	12.73	5.40	-12.86
1981	155.20	122.43	32.77	-101.16	-68.39	6.20	-65.04
1982	149.60	123.07	26.53	-79.88	-53.35	6.00	-64.44

[a]*Source:* USDA (1983), pp. 14, 125 (excluding farm households).

Appendix Table 10.F Expense Items, U.S. Farm Sector, 1950–1982 (billion dollars in nominal prices)

Year	Materials and Taxes[a]	Depreciation[a]	Labor		Imputed Interest on			Total
			Hired[a]	Imputed Operators[a]	Working Capital	Debt Financing Fixed Assets	Equity Financing Current Assets	
1950	11.80	2.30	2.80	7.60	0.68		-0.21	24.97
1951	13.79	2.71	2.90	8.80	0.81		-0.23	28.78
1952	13.99	2.91	2.90	8.90	0.85		-0.24	29.31
1953	12.87	3.03	2.70	8.70	0.71		-0.16	27.84
1954	13.17	3.13	2.60	8.20	0.69		-0.11	27.68
1955	13.48	3.22	2.60	7.90	0.69		-0.11	27.78
1956	13.83	3.27	2.60	7.70	0.67		-0.03	28.04
1957	14.57	3.43	2.70	7.00	0.73		-0.01	28.42
1958	16.17	3.53	2.80	6.90	0.74	0.02		30.16
1959	17.46	3.74	2.60	6.90	0.80	0.02		31.53
1960	17.33	3.77	2.80	6.40	0.76	0.14		31.20
1961	18.00	3.80	2.90	6.10	0.72	0.18		31.70
1962	19.19	3.92	3.00	5.80	0.78	0.22		32.90
1963	19.86	4.04	3.10	5.70	0.82	0.28		33.80
1964	19.60	4.20	3.10	5.40	0.79	0.36		33.45

1965	20.74	4.36	3.20	4.80	0.80	0.46	34.36
1966	22.87	4.63	3.30	4.80	0.82	0.53	36.95
1967	23.93	4.97	3.40	5.20	0.93	0.61	39.04
1968	24.45	5.35	3.50	5.30	0.94	0.73	40.27
1969	26.05	5.66	3.70	5.50	1.00	0.78	42.68
1970	27.51	5.89	3.90	5.30	1.13	0.82	44.54
1971	29.47	6.33	3.90	5.60	1.18	0.85	47.33
1972	32.08	6.72	4.10	5.40	1.21	0.94	50.45
1973	40.76	7.54	4.70	5.50	1.43	1.00	60.93
1974	44.37	8.93	5.50	5.90	1.96	0.96	67.61
1975	45.60	10.60	6.00	5.60	2.03	1.26	71.09
1976	50.61	11.79	6.80	5.20	2.08	1.56	78.04
1977	52.74	13.66	7.20	5.50	2.35	1.94	83.38
1978	59.65	14.35	7.50	5.40	2.49	2.46	91.85
1979	71.28	16.12	8.60	5.20	3.51	2.86	107.57
1980	75.60	17.81	9.20	5.40	4.64	3.31	115.94
1981	78.38	19.52	9.10	6.20	5.61	3.62	122.43
1982	77.99	19.81	10.80	4.50	5.89	4.08	123.07

[a]*Source:* USDA (1983), pp. 15, 125 (excluding farm households).

Appendix Table 10.G   Estimates of Income Components, U.S. Farm Sector, 1950–1982 (billion dollars in nominal prices)

Year	USDA-ERS		Proposed Model	
------	Residual Income to Equity	Real Capital Gains	Operating Income	Capital Gains
1950	5.60	5.40	5.73	4.75
1951	6.70	4.20	6.82	2.92
1952	5.60	−3.90	5.59	−4.86
1953	3.60	−2.60	3.76	−2.30
1954	3.60	−2.10	3.72	−2.77
1955	2.70	5.70	3.02	5.19
1956	2.90	5.30	3.26	5.48
1957	3.30	4.40	3.48	3.70
1958	5.50	10.50	5.74	9.52
1959	2.90	1.80	3.27	1.44
1960	4.10	0.20	4.50	−0.60
1961	5.00	6.90	5.40	6.19
1962	5.50	5.70	6.00	4.60
1963	5.40	4.70	5.90	3.54
1964	4.40	7.20	5.15	7.25
1965	7.50	11.90	8.24	10.36
1966	8.50	7.30	9.35	6.57
1967	6.30	4.90	7.16	3.35
1968	6.10	3.80	7.03	2.61
1969	7.80	−0.70	8.92	−2.42
1970	7.80	−0.70	9.16	−2.50
1971	8.00	13.20	9.37	10.72
1972	13.20	28.70	14.75	27.00
1973	28.60	44.00	30.57	41.81
1974	19.90	2.10	22.39	0.13
1975	17.90	37.90	20.51	33.72
1976	11.90	59.30	15.16	59.91
1977	10.50	27.60	14.32	23.84
1978	18.00	64.90	22.85	63.74
1979	22.10	23.50	28.23	13.78
1980	10.40	−4.70	18.06	−10.72
1981	16.50	−75.10	26.57	−101.16
1982	9.60	−60.90	20.53	−79.88

Source: USDA (1983), pp. 125, 126; and Appendix table 10.E. Excluding farm households, after deducting imputed management expense.

ELEVEN

PERFORMANCE OF THE UNITED STATES FARM SECTOR, 1950–1982

The preceding chapter presents corrected series for operating income, capital gains, and other financial statement items for the United States farm sector which differ from published data. These discrepancies necessitate reexamination of the performance of the sector.

The analysis conducted in this chapter relates to the evaluation of performance, the sources of equity formation and withdrawals, input-output trends, and capital formation during the period 1950–1982.

11.1 INDICATORS FOR PERFORMANCE EVALUATION

In order to evaluate the performance of a farm or a sector, time series and cross section income figures should be compared. To eliminate the effect of differences in scale and price level, it is customary to present income figures as ratios; these ratios are called profitability ratios. Usually, several ratios are used to overcome both measurement errors and the limitation caused by the scale of the denominator (assets, sales). The following four indicators are used here for measuring the performance of the United States farm sector:

(1) *Returns to equity* = operating income after deducting management expense divided by equity. This ratio reflects returns to the owners' equity.

(2) *Returns to fixed assets* = operating income after management plus imputed interest on debt financing fixed assets divided by fixed assets at replacement value. This ratio reflects the end result of assets utilization and is not affected by the level of financial leverage. The

imputed interest on working capital (that is, on current assets) and current assets are not included in this ratio because of the specific behavior of interest on working capital during inflation (chapter 3 and section 9.4).

(3) *Profit margins* = operating income before and after management expense divided by gross receipts. These two ratios reflect the intensity and efficiency of inputs used in production.

(4) *Capital margin* = operating income before management expense plus depreciation and imputed interest on debt financing fixed assets, divided by gross receipts. This ratio reflects total returns to capital (net income, depreciation, and interest) as related to gross receipts; therefore it provides an estimate of the elasticity of output to capital (fixed assets).[1] This ratio is not affected by the method of depreciation or by the level of financial leverage.

The limitation of the first two ratios is that the level of the denominator (equity or assets), in the case of the United States farm sector, changes considerably over time as a result of exogenous factors affecting capital gains, mainly holding gains on land. The limitation of the latter two ratios is that the numerator (income) is correlated with the denominator (gross receipts); thus time series fluctuations in the absolute income level are reduced or leveled. While the first two ratios can be used for intersector comparisons, the last two ratios do not suit this purpose because of the variation that exists among the sectors in the levels of capital and materials.

In a period of inflation, changes in price level during the year should be taken into consideration in computing the ratios. Thus, given that income is a year-end variable, the first two ratios should be measured as follows:

$$\frac{(\text{Returns})_t}{(1 + p)(\text{Capital})_{t-1}} \tag{11.1}$$

where Capital = fixed assets or equity,
      p = inflationjrate,
      t, t−1 = closing and opening dates of balance sheet, respectively.

Given that the gross receipts are recorded in year's average prices, the latter two ratios should be approximated as follows:

$$\frac{(\text{Returns})_t}{(1 + p/2)\ \text{Gross receipts}} \tag{11.2}$$

Table 11.1   Profitability Ratios, U.S. Farm Sector, 1950–1982, Average Values
and Dispersion

	After Management[a]			Before Management[a]	
	Returns[b] to Equity	Returns[c] to Fixed Assets	Profit Margin[d]	Profit Margin[d]	Capital Margin[e]
Average (percent)	3.94	3.88	15.58	19.32	30.19
Coefficient of variation[f]	0.38	0.36	0.28	0.23	0.15
Range (percent)	2.2–10.0	2.2–9.3	9.0–30.8	13.2–34.4	22.9–42.9

[a]Imputed cost of management.
[b]Operating income.
[c]Operating income plus imputed interest on debt financing fixed assets.
[d]Operating income to gross receipts.
[e]Operating income plus depreciation and imputed interest on debt financing fixed assets to gross receipts.
[f]Standard deviation divided by the average.

Relations (11.1) and (11.2) are used in computing the profitability ratios for the farm sector, as shown in the next section.

11.2 PRESENTATION OF INCOME INDICATORS FOR 1950–1982

The four profitability ratios described in the preceding section have been applied to the United States farm sector's data for the analyzed period. The average values of these ratios and their dispersion are presented in table 11.1; the ratios for each year are presented in appendix table 11.A.

The average return on equity for the 33 years was 3.9 percent, which was of the same magnitude as the return on fixed assets. This rate is almost double the average inflation-free interest rates on debt (2.14 percent in appendix table 8.A). The average return on assets in the farm sector is slightly lower than the average rate of return on assets in United States industrial and commercial companies (Foster, 1978, p. 59). It should be noted, however, that in the farm sector, there is an additional return on equity—capital gains which were, on the average, approximately 3 percent on equity.

The average profit margin (operating income before management expense divided by gross receipts) for the 33 years, was 19.32 percent (table 11.1). This ratio means that out of every dollar of gross receipts, about $0.19 on the average is left as operating income to pay for the

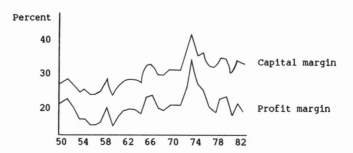

Fig. 11.1 Profitability ratios, based on operating income before management expense, U.S. farm sector (appendix table 11.A)

services of management and equity. The average value of the same ratio after management expense is 15.58 percent (appendix table 11.A). This ratio is much higher than the corresponding ratio in other American business sectors, partially because agriculture is capital intensive.

The average ratio of capital margin (operating income before management expense plus depreciation and real interest on debt financing fixed assets divided by gross receipts) was 30.19 percent. That is, out of every dollar of gross receipts about $0.19 is left as operating income and about $0.11 is left for depreciation and real interest on debt financing fixed assets.

The trend of two of the profitability ratios (profit margin and capital margin before management expense) over the analyzed period are presented in figure 11.1. As can be seen, except for the peak in the years 1972–1975, the ratios are more or less constant. There is, however, an increasing trend in the capital margin ratio over the analyzed period because this margin must cover depreciation charges that increased during the period as a result of the capital (depreciable assets) deepening process which occurred in this period (see next section).

The figures in appendix table 11.A show that the profitability ratios are highly correlated but that there are considerable fluctuations in the ratios over the analyzed period. These fluctuations are measured by the coefficient of variation (standard deviation divided by the average) and by the range (the extreme observations), as shown at the foot of table 11.1. The level of fluctuations in the ratios of profit margin is considerably lower than that of the ratio of returns on equity and on assets (coefficients of variation of about 0.25 and 0.37,

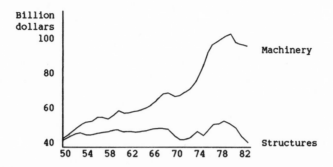

Fig. 11.2 Level of two groups of fixed assets,
in January 1983 prices, U.S. farm sector
(appendix table 10.D)

respectively). The level of fluctuations in the ratio of capital margin
is much lower.

11.3 TRENDS IN INPUT-OUTPUT RELATIONS

The technological changes in agricultural production can be evaluated
by the trends in the usage of the main inputs—assets, labor, and
materials. The usage of assets is measured here by the capital output
ratio; that is, the ratio of assets to gross receipts.[2] The usage of the
inputs, in monetary terms, is measured here by the following three
ratios, where in all the ratios the expenses are related to gross
receipts—labor (hired and operator's imputed cost), depreciation, and
materials (materials, taxes, and imputed interest on working capital).[3]
These ratios indicate the final outcome of the change in physical
usage and the changes in the specific price levels.

The figures in table 10.4 indicate that the value of both structures
and livestock, in constant prices (using the Consumer Price Index),
did not change between 1950 and 1982, whereas the value of the
machinery and the value of investment in cooperatives increased
considerably, in constant prices, in the same period (2.34- and 3.08-
fold, respectively). The trend of the value of depreciable assets
(structures and machinery), in constant prices, over the analyzed
period, is depicted in figure 11.2. As the value of machinery increased
considerably while the level of structures remained more or less stable,
the weight of machinery in the depreciation charges has been dominant,
especially since 1974. It should be noted that the specific price index
of machinery increased more than the Consumer Price Index in this
period; the respective increase in the period 1974–1982 was 2.8- and

Table 11.2   Capital Output Ratios, U.S. Farm Sector, Selected Years, Ratios of Assets to Gross Receipts

	1950	1960	1970	1980	1983
Total assets	3.45	4.70	4.98	6.90	6.67
Total assets excluding land	1.67	1.82	1.65	1.74	1.77
Fixed assets, excluding land	1.09	1.34	1.22	1.31	1.38

Note: Assets at beginning of year, inflated by one half of the year's inflation rate. Excluding farm households.

2.2-fold, respectively. On the other hand, the specific price index of structures was very close to the Consumer Price Index. This means that the trend in the physical volume of machinery was not as steep as suggested by the graph in figure 11.2.

In agricultural production, there is a problem regarding assets to be included in the capital output ratio, particularly in the case of land. To provide further information, three capital output ratios are calculated for the farm sector; these are presented in table 11.2 for selected years. As a result of the tremendous increase in land values, the ratio of total assets to gross receipts doubled during the period 1950–1980, but after 1980 it started to decline. The ratio of fixed assets (excluding land) to gross receipts indicates an increasing trend, especially from 1970 on, resulting from the significant increase in the value of machinery, as shown below. On the other hand, the relative share of current assets declined (table 10.3), thus, the sum of the fixed and current assets (excluding land) relative to gross receipts was more or less stable over the analyzed period.

Three input-output ratios for the United States farm sector for 1950–1982 are presented in appendix table 11.B; average figures for selected groups of years are presented in table 11.3. The use of labor, as measured by the ratio of labor including operators' to gross receipts, decreased during the analyzed period by approximately 70 percent (from a ratio of 32 percent in the early 1950s to a ratio of 10 percent in the early 1980s), whereas the ratio of depreciable assets (mainly machinery) and materials increased in the same period by 63 percent and 40 percent, respectively.

The figures in table 11.3 indicate that the total cost (excluding interest on debt financing fixed assets) in relation to gross receipts is relatively constant in the United States farm sector—close to 80 percent. Only the relative share of the costs has changed—the share

Table 11.3   Average Input-Output Ratios, U.S. Farm Sector, Selected Years

	Ratios (percent)				Growth 1980–82/
	1950–52	1960–62	1970–72	1980–82	1950–52
Labor to gross receipts	32	23	16	10	0.31
Depreciation to gross receipts	8	10	11	13	1.63
Materials to gross receipts	40	49	52	56	1.40
Depreciation and materials	48	59	63	69	
Total	80	82	79	79	

Source: Appendix table 11.B.

of labor cost decreased while the share of depreciation and materials increased, indicating substitution of machinery and materials for labor.

A closer look at the trend of the three input-output ratios is presented in figures 11.3 and 11.4. Figure 11.3 shows that the ratio of depreciation to gross receipts increased during the analyzed period from about 8 percent in 1950 to about 13 percent in 1982, indicating greater utilization of services on depreciable assets. The ratio of labor to gross receipts, on the other hand, indicates an opposite trend. It is interesting to note that since the early 1970s, the two ratios are more or less constant and are close to one another—in the range of 10 percent to 13 percent (see also appendix table 11.B).

The use of materials (materials, taxes, and interest on working capital) in monetary terms, as measured by the third ratio, is depicted in figure 11.4. This ratio increased through the analyzed period, with the most significant increase occurring in the 1950s.

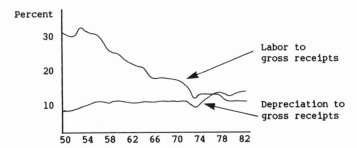

Fig. 11.3 Labor and depreciation ratios, U.S. farm sector (appendix table 11.B)

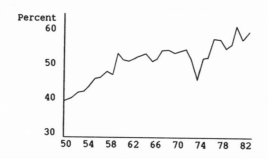

Fig. 11.4 Inputs (materials, taxes and
interest on working capital) to gross
receipts, U.S. farm sector

The end results of the structural changes in the production function
of the United States farm sector, as shown above, are calculated here
through two measures: (1) labor productivity, measured by relating
output (gross receipts inflated by the index of prices received by
farmers for all products) to labor cost (hired and operators' labor
costs inflated by the index of wage rates); and (2) total productivity,
measured by relating output to input (total cost including imputed
interest, before management, as calculated in chapter 10, and inflated
by the index of prices paid by farmers). The growth in these measures
and the variables that are included in these measures, over the
analyzed time span, are presented in table 11.4. (The annual figures
are presented in appendix table 11.C.)

The figures in table 11.4 show that while the Consumer Price Index
showed a four-fold increase in the 32-year period, the index of prices
received by farmers increased by a factor of about 2.5, indicating a
decline in the relative prices received by farmers. The index of prices
paid by farmers, on the other hand, increased at the same pace as
the Consumer Price Index. The squeeze between the index of prices
received and the index of prices paid by farmers did not have a
significant effect on the sector's profitability (appendix table 11.A)
because of the corresponding increase in productivity. In other words,
the benefit stemming from the growth in total productivity of a factor
of about 1.7 in the analyzed period has been transferred from the
farm sector to other sectors. The termendous eight-fold increase in
labor productivity during the period is to a large extent the result
of substitution between labor and the inputs of machinery and
materials, as noted earlier in this section.

Table 11.4   Growth in Productivity Measures and Related Indexes, U.S. Farm Sector, 1982/1950

	Growth Factor	Annual Growth (percent)
Price indexes		
Consumer price index	4.00	4.43
Index of prices received	2.38	2.75
Index of prices paid	4.22	4.60
Index of wage rates	6.41	5.81
Volume indexes		
Gross receipts (output)	1.97	2.14
Total costs (inputs)	1.17	0.49
Labor costs	0.23	−4.49
Measures		
Labor productivity	8.58	6.95
Total productivity	1.69	1.65

Source: Appendix table 11.C.

11.4 TRENDS IN CAPITAL FORMATION

Capital formation means accumulation of capital assets; it is measured by the net investment—gross investment less depreciation. The total capital formation in the United States farm sector during the period was about $70 billion in January 1983 prices (for source, see table 11.5). In comparison, the increase in the total replacement value of fixed assets, between January 1950 and January 1983 was about $76 billion (table 10.4), indicating that total holding gains on fixed assets excluding land were negligible.

The trend of capital formation during the analyzed period is shown in figure 11.5, where the ratios of gross investment and of depreciation, both related to gross receipts, are illustrated (the corresponding figures are presented in appendix table 11.B). The gap between the two curves in figure 11.5 indicates that in the period 1950–1979 capital was formed in most years. In the early 1950s and during the years 1973–1979, capital formation was especially high, but in 1980 the trend changed towards a negative capital formation.

Some more detailed data on capital formation during the ten-year period 1973–1982 are presented in table 11.5, where the annual formation of capital is presented alongside the inflation-free interest

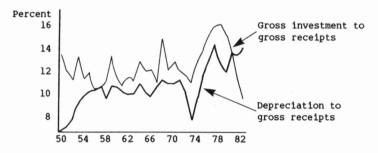

Fig. 11.5 Depreciation and investment
ratios, U.S. farm sector (appendix table 11.B)

rates. Between 1973 and 1982, the average annual capital formation was $2.14 billion in January 1983 prices. Between 1973 and 1979, ignoring the years 1980–1982, the average annual figure was $4.6 billion.

The figures in table 11.5 show the well-known phenomenon wherein the capital formation is negatively correlated with inflation-free interest rate.[4] In four of the years, when the inflation-free rate was negative, annual capital formation was at least $5 billion; when the inflation-

Table 11.5 Capital Formation in the U.S. Farm Sector, 1973–1982 (billion dollars in 1982 prices)

	Depreciation	Gross Investment	Capital Formation[a]	Real Interest Rate[b] (percent)
1973	16.3	22.1	5.8	−2.05
1974	17.4	22.4	5.0	−3.49
1975	19.0	22.2	3.2	0.99
1976	20.0	23.6	3.6	2.72
1977	21.7	23.9	2.2	1.20
1978	21.2	26.5	5.3	−1.04
1979	21.4	26.4	5.0	−4.23
1980	20.8	21.0	0.2	−1.46
1981	20.7	17.8	−2.9	2.83
1982	19.8	13.9	−5.9	7.52
Total			21.4	
Average	19.8	22.0	2.14	0.30

[a]Gross investment less depreciation; based on data from USDA 1983, pp. 15, 19.
[b]Inflation-free rate on total loans (Appendix table 8.A).

free interest rate started to rise in 1980, the level of capital formation declined in tandem with the rise in the level of the interest rate. In other words, the level of the real interest rate, which has been affected by inflation (section 8.2), affected the level of capital formation.

The negative capital formation in 1981 and 1982 can be explained by the significant increase in the real interest rate (which also affected the profitability of the United States farm sector), and by the increase in the financial burden. The latter was caused by the deterioration of the financial position of the farm sector, a process which was affected considerably by high inflation in the late 1970s (section 8.4).

11.5 EQUITY FORMATION, 1950-1982

One of the outstanding features in the United States farm sector's financial position is the huge accumulation of equity since World War II. The total value of equity increased, in January 1983 prices, from approximately \$400 billion in January 1950 to a peak of approximately \$950 billion in January 1980, and then declined sharply to about \$750 billion in January 1983 (table 10.3).

This accumulation of equity can be attributed to three factors: (1) the relative high level of annual operating income; (2) the high level of annual capital gains, mainly holding gains on land; and (3) equity additions or withdrawals, on which there are no available data. In this section an attempt is made to estimate the share of these three factors in the accumulation of equity, over the analyzed period.

The total amount of operating income (after deducting management expense) over the period 1950-1982 was \$765 billion in January 1983 prices (appendix table 11.D). This sum has been generated by \$392 billion equity in 1950 (in January 1983 prices). In other words, the annual rate of return generated by the United States farm sector, after charging imputed cost of operators' labor and management, was

$$\sqrt[32]{\frac{765 + 392}{392}} - 1 = 0.0344 = 3.44\%$$

The total cumulative amount of capital gains in the period 1950-1982 was \$485 billion in January 1983 prices. (Out of this sum, holding gains on land accounted for \$443 billion—table 10.5.) The annual rate of return of both operating income after management expense and capital gains, on the \$392 billion equity in 1950, was 4.58 percent—that is, about one percentage point above the return from operating income.

Equity formation in a given year can be stated as follows:

$$E_t - (1 + p)E_{t-1} = OI_M + CG + \text{Addition} \qquad (11.3)$$

where E = equity,

$t, t-1$ = closing and opening dates of balance sheet, respectively,

p = inflation rate,

OI_M = operating income, after management,

CG = capital gains.

In other words, equity addition in a given year is

$$\text{Addition} = E_t - (1 + p)E_{t-1} - OI_M - CG \qquad (11.4)$$

Considering operating income (after operators' labor and management) as dividends which can be withdrawn from the firm without impairing its financial position, then the net change in equity (new issues or withdrawals) is defined as

$$\text{Net equity change} = E_t - (1+p)\, E_{t-1} - CG \qquad (11.5)$$

Applying relation (11.5) to the United States farm sector's data shows the amount of operating income that has been retained in the sector (a positive net change) or the amount of equity that has been withdrawn from the sector over and above the operating income (a negative net change). The results for 1982 are:

$$\text{Net equity change} = 744.9 - (1 + 0.035448)\ 791.2$$
$$- (-79.9) = \$5.5 \text{ billion}$$

The significance of this figure is that in 1982, out of the $20.5 billion operating income after management, $5.5 billion has been retained and the rest has been withdrawn from the sector. Net equity changes for every year in the analyzed period 1950–1982, in constant prices, are presented in appendix table 11.D.

The net equity change for the entire period 1950–1982, in constant prices, is −$132 billion. The main portion of this sum was withdrawn during the period 1974–1980, when the inflation rate was high (appendix table 11.D). These withdrawals of equity were substituted by loans.[5] It is interesting to note that the trend of equity withdrawal stopped in 1980, and in the two years 1981 and 1982, equity was added—that is, a portion of the operating income was retained. The high real interest rates and the decline in land values may explain this shift in the trend of equity withdrawal.

NOTES

1. See, e.g., Shumway, Talpaz, and Beattie (1979).

2. The ratio of assets to gross receipts is calculated by inflating the assets' value at the beginning of the year by one-half of the year's inflation rate.

3. The reason for including interest on working capital in this ratio is that it complements historical cost of materials, as shown in chapters 2 and 3.

4. For similar results see a recent study by Lamm (1982).

5. From the accounting point of view, the cumulative values of the individual items on both sides of the balance sheet (equity, debt, fixed and current assets) should be balanced. This would not hold for a deflated series of balance sheet items because loans are not deflated. Hence, the cumulative series of assets and liabilities would not balance.

Appendix Table 11.A   Profitability Ratios, U.S. Farm Sector, 1950–1982 (percent)

Year	After Management[a] Return[b] to Equity	After Management[a] Return[c] to Fixed Assets	After Management[a] Profit Margin[d]	After Management[a] Capital Margin[e]	Before Management[a] Profit Margin[d]	Before Management[a] Capital Margin[e]
1950	5.60	5.81	17.24	18.76	20.85	27.20
1951	5.90	6.12	18.04	19.30	21.75	28.33
1952	4.52	4.62	15.34	17.98	19.18	26.53
1953	3.11	3.12	11.35	14.49	15.28	23.95
1954	3.26	3.27	11.43	14.77	15.42	24.68
1955	2.55	2.53	9.41	12.52	13.16	22.88
1956	2.62	2.61	9.87	12.51	13.51	23.33
1957	2.61	2.61	10.31	13.83	14.16	24.28
1958	4.17	4.16	15.28	19.60	19.01	28.47
1959	2.17	2.18	9.01	14.58	12.59	22.94
1960	2.95	2.95	12.05	18.57	15.79	26.25
1961	3.56	3.53	13.95	21.42	17.82	28.11
1962	3.78	3.75	14.77	22.45	18.46	28.61
1963	3.60	3.56	14.18	22.12	18.03	28.40
1964	3.06	3.06	12.78	21.43	16.50	27.81
1965	4.71	4.57	18.43	26.64	22.23	32.99
1966	4.92	4.74	19.14	26.88	22.82	33.34
1967	3.58	3.51	14.70	22.93	18.39	29.77
1968	3.33	3.28	14.04	22.43	17.81	29.82
1969	3.96	3.84	16.22	24.31	19.84	31.41
1970	3.94	3.83	16.06	24.01	19.73	31.37
1971	3.96	3.85	15.69	23.41	19.37	31.31
1972	5.76	5.45	21.45	28.44	25.07	36.13
1973	9.96	9.26	30.79	35.76	34.40	42.89
1974	5.74	5.51	22.69	27.80	26.33	36.20
1975	5.26	5.02	20.87	26.49	24.73	36.68
1976	3.41	3.35	15.33	21.48	19.05	32.41
1977	2.74	2.75	13.75	20.21	17.46	32.20
1978	3.89	3.75	18.46	24.54	22.14	35.43
1979	3.84	3.71	18.92	24.33	22.50	34.83
1980	2.18	2.24	12.47	18.47	16.13	30.20
1981	3.03	3.00	16.60	22.58	20.43	34.57
1982	2.52	2.57	13.56	20.55	17.50	33.08
Average	3.94	3.88	15.58	21.38	19.32	30.19

[a]Imputed cost of management.
[b]Operating income.
[c]Operating income plus imputed interest on debt financing fixed assets.
[d]Operating income to gross receipts.
[e]Operating income plus depreciation and imputed interest on debt financing fixed assets to gross receipts.

Appendix Table 11.B   Input-Output Ratios, U.S. Farm Sector, 1950–1982, Inputs Related to Gross Receipts (percent)

Year	Labor[a]	Depreciation	Materials[b]	Investment[c]
1950	32.60	7.21	39.12	12.64
1951	31.62	7.33	39.45	11.50
1952	32.51	8.02	40.88	10.79
1953	34.65	9.21	41.27	12.49
1954	33.03	9.57	42.38	10.98
1955	32.81	10.06	44.28	11.29
1956	31.69	10.06	44.62	10.06
1957	29.22	10.33	46.07	10.20
1958	26.01	9.46	45.34	10.70
1959	26.32	10.35	50.60	12.55
1960	24.80	10.17	48.75	10.79
1961	23.32	9.85	48.48	10.37
1962	21.78	9.69	49.42	11.07
1963	21.31	9.79	50.06	10.83
1964	21.20	10.48	50.85	12.08
1965	18.06	9.84	48.63	11.51
1966	16.84	9.62	49.26	11.57
1967	17.92	10.35	51.80	10.61
1968	17.89	10.87	51.61	13.89
1969	17.16	10.55	50.46	11.59
1970	16.49	10.56	51.32	12.17
1971	16.13	10.75	52.04	11.53
1972	14.03	9.93	49.18	11.05
1973	10.73	7.93	44.37	10.70
1974	12.18	9.54	49.50	12.23
1975	12.16	11.12	49.92	12.98
1976	12.38	12.17	54.37	14.41
1977	12.50	13.44	54.22	14.78
1978	10.81	12.03	52.09	15.04
1979	9.77	11.42	52.97	14.08
1980	10.47	12.77	57.55	12.88
1981	9.86	12.58	54.12	10.84
1982	10.23	13.24	56.07	9.32
Average	20.26	10.31	48.82	11.80

[a]Labor expenses (hired and operators' imputed cost) to gross receipts.
[b]Materials, taxes, and interest on working capital to gross receipts.
[c]Gross investment.

Appendix Table 11.C Measures of Productivity and Related Variables, U.S. Farm Sector, 1950–1982

Year	Specific Price Indexes[a]			Volume Indexes[b]			Productivity	
	Prices Received	Prices Paid	Wage Rates	Gross Receipts	Total Costs	Labor Costs	Labor[c]	Total[d]
1950	56	37	22	75.76	105.27	66.65	1.14	0.72
1951	66	41	25	74.56	109.49	65.99	1.13	0.68
1952	63	42	26	76.63	108.88	63.99	1.20	0.70
1953	56	40	27	78.14	108.58	59.53	1.31	0.72
1954	54	40	27	80.54	107.94	56.40	1.43	0.75
1955	51	40	27	83.45	108.36	54.83	1.52	0.77
1956	50	40	28	86.45	109.36	51.87	1.67	0.79
1957	51	42	29	86.58	105.54	47.16	1.84	0.82
1958	55	43	30	90.20	109.43	45.59	1.98	0.82
1959	53	43	32	90.59	114.37	41.86	2.16	0.79
1960	52	44	33	94.89	110.61	39.31	2.41	0.86
1961	53	44	33	96.86	112.39	38.45	2.52	0.86
1962	53	45	34	101.38	114.04	36.49	2.78	0.89
1963	53	45	35	103.64	117.17	35.45	2.92	0.88
1964	52	45	36	102.56	115.97	33.29	3.08	0.88
1965	54	47	38	109.11	114.06	29.68	3.68	0.96
1966	58	49	41	110.30	117.65	27.86	3.96	0.94
1967	55	49	44	116.07	124.30	27.56	4.21	0.93
1968	56	51	48	116.85	123.17	25.85	4.52	0.95
1969	59	53	53	120.83	125.62	24.48	4.94	0.96
1970	60	55	57	123.69	126.34	22.76	5.44	0.98

1971	62	58	59	126.35	127.30	22.70	5.57	0.99
1972	69	62	63	130.49	126.93	21.26	6.14	1.03
1973	98	71	69	129.06	133.88	20.84	6.19	0.96
1974	105	81	79	118.56	130.21	20.35	5.83	0.91
1975	101	89	85	125.63	124.61	19.24	6.53	1.01
1976	102	95	93	126.35	128.14	18.19	6.94	0.99
1977	100	100	100	135.13	130.08	17.91	7.55	1.04
1978	115	108	107	137.97	132.68	17.00	8.12	1.04
1979	132	123	117	142.27	136.43	16.63	8.55	1.04
1980	134	138	127	138.36	131.07	16.21	8.54	1.06
1981	139	150	137	148.50	127.33	15.75	9.43	1.17
1982	133	156	141	149.60	123.07	15.30	9.78	1.22
Growth	2.38	4.22	6.41	1.97	1.17	0.23	8.60	1.69

aSource: Agricultural Statistics 1982, 1983.
bGross receipts (appendix table 10.E), total costs (appendix table 10.F) and labor costs (appendix table 10.F) in nominal prices deflated by the specific price indexes, respectively.
cGross receipts to labor costs, in constant dollars.
dGross receipts to total costs, in constant dollars.

Appendix Table 11.D   Equity Formation, U.S. Farm Sector, 1950–1982 (billion dollars in January 1982 prices)

Year	Inflation Rate	Annual Figures Operating Income After Management	Capital Gains	Net Equity Change	Cumulative Figures Capital Gains	Net Equity Change
1950	7.94	22.00	18.24	15.09	18.24	15.09
1951	4.20	25.14	10.74	16.67	28.99	31.76
1952	0.63	20.45	− 17.79	1.78	11.19	33.54
1953	1.13	13.60	− 8.34	− 11.74	2.86	21.80
1954	− 0.74	13.58	− 10.09	24.15	− 7.24	45.96
1955	0.25	10.97	18.87	− 10.13	11.64	35.83
1956	3.11	11.50	19.33	− 4.02	30.97	31.81
1957	3.50	11.88	12.61	− 3.80	43.58	28.01
1958	1.28	19.31	32.03	4.84	75.61	32.84
1959	1.27	10.88	4.79	− 5.40	80.40	27.44
1960	1.59	14.73	− 1.96	− 4.24	78.45	23.20
1961	0.67	17.55	20.10	− 4.55	98.54	18.65
1962	1.33	19.25	14.76	− 5.76	113.31	12.89
1963	1.65	18.61	11.16	− 4.10	124.47	8.79
1964	1.08	16.07	22.64	− 11.71	147.11	− 2.92
1965	1.92	25.21	31.72	− 3.57	178.83	− 6.49
1966	3.35	27.69	19.47	− 9.05	198.30	− 15.53
1967	3.45	20.50	9.60	− 2.98	207.90	− 18.52
1968	4.61	19.25	7.15	− 4.29	215.06	− 22.81
1969	6.19	23.00	− 6.24	− 6.65	208.82	− 29.46
1970	5.21	22.44	− 6.12	− 2.31	202.70	− 31.77
1971	3.36	22.22	25.42	− 1.02	228.12	− 32.79
1972	3.65	33.74	61.76	− 5.83	289.88	− 38.62
1973	9.40	63.92	87.41	2.86	377.29	− 35.75
1974	11.74	41.89	0.24	− 48.30	377.53	− 84.05
1975	6.79	35.94	59.08	0.37	436.61	− 83.69
1976	5.16	25.27	99.82	− 21.89	536.43	− 105.57
1977	6.73	22.35	37.22	− 13.40	573.66	− 118.97
1978	9.41	32.60	90.96	− 6.21	664.61	− 125.18
1979	13.97	35.34	17.25	− 4.47	681.87	− 129.66
1980	11.74	20.23	− 12.01	− 17.75	669.85	− 147.41
1981	8.21	27.51	− 104.75	9.60	565.11	− 137.81
1982	3.54	20.53	− 79.88	5.53	485.23	− 132.28
Total		765.14	485.23	− 132.28		
Average		23.19	14.70	− 4.01		

Appendix Table 11.E   Consumer Price Indexes, U.S., January 1950–January 1983

| | January Index | | | | Year's Average Index | | |
Year	CPI	1950 Base	Annual Rate	Inflating Factor	CPI	1950 Base	Annual Rate	Inflating Factor
1950	70.50	100	7.94	4.14	72.10	100	7.91	4.00
1951	76.10	108	4.20	3.84	77.80	108	2.19	3.71
1952	79.30	112	0.63	3.68	79.50	110	0.75	3.63
1953	79.80	113	1.13	3.66	80.10	111	0.50	3.60
1954	80.70	114	−0.74	3.62	80.50	112	−0.37	3.59
1955	80.10	114	0.25	3.65	80.20	111	1.50	3.60
1956	80.30	114	3.11	3.64	81.40	113	3.56	3.55
1957	82.80	117	3.50	3.53	84.30	117	2.73	3.42
1958	85.70	122	1.28	3.41	86.60	120	0.81	3.33
1959	86.80	123	1.27	3.37	87.30	121	1.60	3.31
1960	87.90	125	1.59	3.32	88.70	123	1.01	3.25
1961	89.30	127	0.67	3.27	89.60	124	1.12	3.22
1962	89.90	128	1.33	3.25	90.60	126	1.21	3.19
1963	91.10	129	1.65	3.21	91.70	127	1.31	3.15
1964	92.60	131	1.08	3.15	92.90	129	1.72	3.11
1965	93.60	133	1.92	3.12	94.50	131	2.86	3.05
1966	95.40	135	3.35	3.06	97.20	135	2.88	2.97
1967	98.60	140	3.45	2.96	100.00	139	4.20	2.89
1968	102.00	145	4.61	2.86	104.20	145	5.37	2.77
1969	106.70	151	6.19	2.74	109.80	152	5.92	2.63
1970	113.30	161	5.21	2.58	116.30	161	4.30	2.48
1971	119.20	169	3.36	2.45	121.30	168	3.30	2.38
1972	123.20	175	3.65	2.37	125.30	174	6.23	2.30
1973	127.70	181	9.40	2.29	133.10	185	10.97	2.17
1974	139.70	198	11.74	2.09	147.70	205	9.14	1.95
1975	156.10	221	6.79	1.87	161.20	224	5.77	1.79
1976	166.70	236	5.16	1.75	170.50	236	6.45	1.69
1977	175.30	249	6.73	1.67	181.50	252	7.60	1.59
1978	187.10	265	9.41	1.56	195.30	271	11.47	1.48
1979	204.70	290	13.97	1.43	217.70	302	13.46	1.33
1980	233.30	331	11.74	1.25	247.00	343	10.24	1.17
1981	260.70	370	8.21	1.12	272.30	378	5.99	1.06
1982	282.10	400	3.54	1.04	288.60	400		1.00
1983	292.10	414	3.63	1.00				

Note: All items, wage earners, and clerical workers, revised (CPI-W).
Source: U.S. Department of Commerce, *Business Statistics and Survey of Current Business Conditions.*

TWELVE

CONCLUSIONS:
IMPLICATIONS FOR POLICY

Many pitfalls encountered by businessmen and analysts are the result of the incorrect treatment of interest expense in conducting financial analyses under inflationary conditions. The interest rate under inflation embodies compensation on the loss of the loan's purchasing power. This element is not a cost but rather should be considered as accelerated repayment on the principal. As a consequence, the true estimates of costs and income and the composition of liabilities (equity, short- and long-term loans) are affected.

Interest costs increase during inflation, usually by more than the inflation factor. For example, during the 33-year period 1950–1982, the level of loans of the United States farm sector rose, in real terms, by a factor of 4.4 while the interest bill rose, also in real terms, by a factor of 9.4. The average inflation rate during that period was 4.4 percent per annum. Although not all the interest outlay is a cost, it must be paid, and for this reason the liquidity position of the firm is impaired.

The following policy implications can be drawn from the impact of inflation on the financial activities of business, under existing tax rules and financing practices:

INCOME PERFORMANCE

The model for income measurement as developed in Part IV differs considerably from the USDA-ERS model (and also from the FASB), especially as regards the estimation of operating income (which is under the firm's control) and capital gains; although the total income arrived at by these models is similar. Generally, published data regarding these two income components should be approached with caution. The main difference lies in the allocation of interest expense in calculating operating income and capital gains.

PRICING AND COSTING

The simple rule to follow in costing and pricing is to charge inflation-free interest on the replacement value of fixed assets alongside current cost depreciation, and to charge nominal interest rates on other assets (inventories and monetary assets) alongside other recorded (unadjusted) input costs.

The practice of charging nominal interest and current cost depreciation on all assets double counts the inflation factor in costing, the consequence of which is an undue rise in prices, which in turn accelerates the inflationary process.

INTEREST ON WORKING CAPITAL

The importance of correctly estimating the firm's interest on working capital in costing and in income measurement has been illustrated in parts II and IV. For the United States farm sector in general, interest on working capital can be estimated as the product of two terms: the market interest rate and three quarters of current assets. This rule of thumb may be useful for policymakers in assessing farm cost budgets and farm operating income.

FUNDS FOR CURRENT ASSETS

The value of current assets, which finance working capital, increases proportionately with inflation. Hence, when these assets are financed by loans, there is a problem for the firm in raising additional funds in order to maintain their purchasing power value. The problem of financing current assets is especially serious when the firm is growing and when inflation is high and persistent.

FUNDS FOR INVESTMENT

Proper financing of investments requires matching the terms of finance to those of the investment. In other words, investment in fixed assets should be financed by equity and/or by long-term loans. In chapter 5, we illustrated that in times of inflation, the liquidity position of the firm deteriorates through the substitution of short-term for long-term loans. The remedy for this problem is to introduce the practice of loan indexation for long-term investments (chapter 6).

FINANCIAL LIQUIDITY

Under existing income tax rules, firms are induced to substitute equity by loans in order to eliminate and avoid equity erosion. This induces firms to increase financial leverage. Furthermore, under existing financing practices (no loan indexation), long-term loans are automatically converted to short-term loans, causing financial stress. This scenario has occurred in the United States farm sector in the last decade: the level of loans per one dollar of gross receipts increased from 90 percent in 1970 to 128 percent in 1982; the ratio of non-real estate loans to real estate loans increased from 87 percent in 1970 to 101 percent in 1982; and the cash income to one dollar receipts declined from 33 percent in 1970 to 19 percent in 1982.

The remedy for this problem is reconstruction of loans; that is, short-term loans financing fixed assets should be converted to long-term indexed loans.

EFFECT OF INFLATION ON TAXATION

The general view is that under existing tax rules, inflation causes overtaxation. This is true in the case of equity finance. However, the process of equity erosion induces firms to increase the share of loan financing. In chapter 7, we illustrated the fact that beyond a given level of financial leverage, the firm reaps a net tax benefit which leads to undertaxation. When the inflationary process is persistent, the end result is undertaxation of the business economy.

The preceding taxation effect and the practice of price-setting firms in double counting the inflation factor may explain the failure that many countries experience in attempting to curb inflation.

REFERENCES

Aharoni, Y., and T. Ophir. 1967. "Accounting for Linked Loans." *Journal of Accounting Research,* Spring, pp. 1–26.

Bailey, E. L., ed. 1978. *Pricing Practices and Strategies.* New York: The Conference Board. Reprinted, Amsterdam: Elsevier Science, 1983.

Barry, P. J., J. A. Hopkins, and C. B. Baker. 1983. *Financial Management in Agriculture,* 3rd ed. Danville, Ill.: Interstate Printers and Publishers.

Board of Governors of the Federal Reserve System. 1984. *Balance Sheets of the U.S. Economy 1945–1983.* Washington, D.C. April.

Darby, M. R. 1975. "The Financial and Tax Effects of Monetary Policy on Interest Rates." *Economic Inquiry* 13(June):266–76.

Enthoven, A.J.H. 1982. *Current Value Accounting—Its Concepts and Practice at N.V. Philips Industries, The Netherlands.* Dallas, Tex.: Center for International Accounting Development, University of Texas.

Feldstein, M., and L. Summers. 1978. "Inflation, Tax Rules, and the Long-Term Interest Rate." *Brookings Papers on Economic Activity,* No. 1, pp. 61–99.

Financial Accounting Standards Board (FASB). 1979. *Statement of Financial Accounting Standards No. 33—Financial Reporting and Changing Prices.* Stamford, Conn.

Foster, G. 1978. *Financial Statement Analysis.* Englewood Cliffs, N.J.: Prentice-Hall.

Goldschmidt, Y., and L. Shashua. 1984. "Distortion of Income by FASB Statement No. 33." *Journal of Accounting, Auditing and Finance.* Fall, pp. 54–67.

Hill, G. P. 1984. "Measuring Farm Income under Conditions of Inflation: The Gains from Borrowing." *Journal of Agricultural Economics,* January, pp. 51–60.

Hottel, J. B., and C. D. Evans. 1980. "Returns to Equity Capital in the U.S. Farm Production Sector." *Balance Sheet of the Farming Sector, Supplement,* AIB-430. Washington, D.C.: ESCS, USDA. Pp. 51–62.

Institute of Chartered Accountants in England and Wales. 1980. *Statement of Standard Accounting Practice No. 16: Current Cost Accounting.* London: Accounting Standards Committee, Accountancy Bodies.

Kellison, S. G. 1970. *The Theory of Interest.* Homewood, Ill.: Irwin.

Lamm, McFall R., Jr. 1982. "Investment in Agriculture—An Empirical Analysis." *Agricultural Finance Review,* October, pp. 16–23.

Leuthold, S. C. 1981. "Interest Rates, Inflation and Deflation." *Financial Analyst Journal,* January-February, pp. 28–41.

Melichar, E. 1979. "Capital Gains versus Current Income in the Farming Sector." *American Journal of Agricultural Economics* 61(December):1085–92.

——. 1984. "A Financial Perspective on Agriculture." *Federal Reserve Bulletin,* January, pp. 1–13.

Modigliani, F., and R. A. Cohn. 1979. "Inflation, Rational Valuation and the Market." *Financial Analyst Journal* 35 (March-April):24–44.

Morris, W. T. 1960. *Engineering Economics.* Homewood, Ill.: Irwin.

Penson, J. B., Jr., and D. A. Lins. 1980. *Agricultural Finance: An Introduction to Micro and Macro Concepts.* Englewood Cliffs, N.J.: Prentice Hall.

Shashua, L., and Y. Goldschmidt. 1983. *Tools for Financial Management—Emphasis on Inflation.* Lexington, Mass.: Lexington Books.

——. 1984. "Costing Depreciable Assets' Services during Inflation." *The Engineering Economist* 30, 2:157–171.

——. 1985. "The Specific Role of Interest in Financial and Economic Analysis under Inflation: Real, Nominal or a Combination of Both," *American Journal of Agricultural Economics* 67, 2(May).

Shashua, L., Y. Goldschmidt, and J. S. Hillman. 1983. "The Gearing Adjustment in Current Cost Profit Measurement: Analysis and Clarification." Department of Agricultural Economics, Working Paper No. 22, University of Arizona, Tucson.

Shumway, C. R., H. Talpaz, and B. R. Beattie. 1979. "The Factor Share Approach to Production Function 'Estimation': Actual or Estimated Equilibrium Shares?" *American Journal of Agricultural Economics* 61(August):561–564.

Sundell, P. A. 1983. "The Adjustment of Nominal Interest Rates to Inflation: A Review of Recent Literature." *Agricultural Economic Research* 35(October):15–26.

Symonds, C. W. 1982. *Pricing for Profits.* New York: Amacom, A Division of the American Management Association.

Thompson, J. 1983. "Farm Financial Distress: Nature, Scope, and Measurement of the Problem." *The Agricultural Law Journal,* Winter, pp. 450–474.

Tweeten, L. 1981a. *Farmland Pricing and Cash Flow in an Inflationary Economy.* Research Report P-811. Stillwater, Okla.: Agricultural Experiment Station, Oklahoma State University.

——. 1981b. "A Review of the Impact of Inflation on Agriculture." In Robert Spitze, ed., *Policy Research Notes.* Washington, D.C.: Economic Research Service.

U.S. Department of Agriculture (USDA), Economic Research Service (ERS). 1976. *Balance Sheet of the Farming Sector, Supplement No. 1.* Agriculture Information Bulletin No. 389. Washington, D.C.: Economic Research Service.

——. 1983. *Economic Indicators of the Farm Sector—Income and Balance Sheet Statistics, 1982,* ECIFS 2-2. Washington, D.C.: October.

U.S. Department of Agriculture, Economics, Statistics, and Cooperative Service (ESCS). 1981a. "Firm Enterprise Data System (FEDS)." Stillwater, Okla.: Department of Agricultural Economics, Oklahoma State University.

——. 1981b. *Costs of Producing Selected Crops in the United States 1978, 1979, 1980, and Projections for 1981.* Washington, D.C.: Committee on Agriculture, Nutrition, and Forestry, U.S. Senate, August.

White, D. L. 1981. "Next in Corporate Finance: Index-Linked Loans?" *Harvard Business Review,* September-October, pp. 14–22.

INDEX